THE STREET CHIL

The Street Children of Brazil

One Woman's Remarkable Story

Sarah de Carvalho

Hodder & Stoughton
LONDON SYDNEY AUCKLAND

British Library Cataloguing in Publication Data
A record for this book is available from the British Library

ISBN 0 340 64164 9

Printed and bound in Great Britain by
Clays Ltd, St Ives plc

Hodder and Stoughton
A Division of Hodder Headline Ltd
338 Euston Road
London NW1 3BH
www.madaboutbooks.com

To Colin and Julie Jarman,
my parents.

I would like to acknowledge with deep gratitude and thanks every one of you who is involved with us in this ministry, be it through prayer, financial or voluntary help. 'Happy Child' recognise that because of this partnership we are able to reach out to these lost children and teenagers here in Brazil and share God's love with them.

Contents

1

Borel, Rio de Janeiro: 'I Don't Want to Die!'

I heard the crack of a gunshot. My heart skipped a beat. But it sounded far in the distance from where we were, so I relaxed again, wiping the sweat off my brow. My head felt as if it would burst from the heat of the Brazilian afternoon sun.

Suddenly another shot rang out, now louder than the first. I felt my heart beating faster and my mouth was becoming dry. Then two shots, three shots, four shots . . .

'Oh my God,' I heard myself cry out, 'they're coming closer.'

'They're above us, Sarah,' screamed Lila.

'Quick, lie down on the floor,' I shouted back.

The four of us sprawled on the cold mud floor, filling the tiny slum hut. The pressure of someone's body was over my legs, and my head was squashed under the old iron bed, restricting all movement. My heart was racing, my thoughts were running in a hundred different directions.

A bullet whistled over the tin and cardboard roof . . . then from the opposite direction an explosion of bullets rained out from a machinegun in retaliation.

We were caught in the middle of crossfire.

The baby started to cry. I shifted my body and stretched

1

out my left arm, straining to touch him. I reached his small soft foot and held it. He can't die, I pleaded in my thoughts, he's so young.

I could hear someone else crying.

'Sarah,' exclaimed Lila, 'they're all around us.'

'It's the gang from the other *favela* of Casa Branca,' gasped Andre, 'they heard that the police were here this morning and that they managed to arrest some of the leaders and members of Borel's *quadrilha*. Now Casa Branca think it's their opportunity to fight back at their rival enemies here in Borel.'

This was my new home. One of the most dangerous favelas (shantytowns) in the city of Rio de Janeiro. A far cry from my comfortable apartment in London, England.

Stretching itself high up over the side of a mountain, Borel is home for over forty thousand people. From the road below it looks like a mass of hundreds of thousands of different-coloured box houses, some made of painted brick and others of mud and sticks. The desperate poverty protruding its ugly head for all to see is a stark contrast not only to the natural beauty of this *Cidade Maravilhosa* with its beaches, *florestas* and mountainous landscape, but also to the wealth evident in Rio's mansions, smart apartment blocks, shopping malls and hotels: the city of contrasts and extremes.

I had been assured three weeks earlier, when I'd first moved in during the month of July 1991, that there hadn't been any serious shooting for five months.

At the time, I was working with a small team of five young Brazilian missionaries from the international organisation Youth With A Mission. Most of them had lived in

Borel for over a year. We had a much-needed first-aid clinic and a Sunday school in a house which was situated on the main square in the centre of the favela halfway up the steep mountainside. The square was nicknamed *Banco de Sangue* (Bank of Blood) because of all the murders which had taken place on it.

My bedroom was situated on the top floor of a three-storey house belonging to a Christian family who had lived in Borel for three generations. It was positioned on the opposite side of the square to the clinic. I was very fortunate and extremely grateful because the house was made of brick. Each of the three floors in the house consisted of two narrow rooms only, so from the outside it looked tall and tower-like.

My room was rectangular in shape and simple in decoration with a small bed and a cupboard. But I felt very spoilt because the walls were plastered and painted white. It was also full of windows which covered two sides of the four walls, shedding lots of light into the room and allowing a welcome cool breeze to flow in from the coast. There was a glass door, too, which led out on to a balcony giving a good view of the main square and the favela beyond.

However, as I was later to discover, the main square was the direct shooting target for the gangs from rival favelas positioned on the other side of the mountain. And on many a night I was to find myself crawling along the floor below the window line to avoid any flying bullets.

The majority of the 545 favelas in Rio are protected by their own gangs, whose livelihoods are made from the trafficking of drugs and from robberies. The more drugs trafficked, the more powerful and rich the gang. There is, therefore, a lot of rivalry between the favelas and as a result gang warfare and murders. The gangs are like a mafia: extremely tough, well armed and well organised.

High up on the very top of the mountain above Borel there is a large wooden cross, not, I was later to discover, to symbolise the death of Jesus Christ but to symbolise the mark of Commando Vermelho (Red Commander), which is the most dangerous and most powerful mafia of drug trafficking in Rio de Janeiro.

The other room on my floor belonged to Anita. She was the nurse for the clinic and was well accustomed with the goings on in Borel, as she had worked there already for over a year. Our bathroom was tiny and once you entered it you couldn't turn around easily. But the cold-water pipe, which served as our shower, brought a welcome relief to our sweaty, sticky bodies. We were the only two girls in the team; the other four young men, Pedro, Claudio, Geraldo and Ivan, lived above the clinic across the square.

So it was at 6 a.m. on this same day, a Sunday, just three weeks after I had moved in, that we had all been woken up from our sleep by a tirade of shooting and explosions. It had been like a nightmare; I had only heard such weapons used in movies like *Rambo*. And I had tried desperately to muffle the deathly sounds by pressing my pillow around my ears, but to no avail. The armed civil and federal police had entered Borel in the early hours to take the *bandidos* by surprise, and also to prevent as many deaths of other, innocent, residents as possible.

By the afternoon all seemed to have quietened down, so accompanied by two young teenagers, Lila and Andre, both natives of Borel, we had set out to visit Rose, her

4

husband Nilton and their six-month-old baby on the other side of the favela.

Like many attempting to escape from reality, Nilton was an alcoholic. Therefore most of the little he earned went in drink. He had built their tiny home out of wrought-iron scraps, cardboard and red earth. Inside there was only room enough for a small single bed, a chair and a small table with a gas ring where Rose cooked. Water was collected from a communal well.

Their home was situated in an area of the favela, appropriately called A Grotta. This was where the poorest of the poor lived, as it was dangerously positioned on the very outskirts between Borel and the neighbouring favela, Casa Branca. The people living there were the victims of the majority of the shooting.

Rose was suffering from bad leg infections caused by uncleaned cuts and mosquito bites, so I had brought some first aid with me. Infections were a constant problem in the favelas, encouraged by the open sewers and the waste and litter which piled up by the sides of the pathways between the slum homes. The heat of the tropical sun by midday often made the stench of defecation and rotting litter unbearable.

As the three of us had carefully made our way single file along narrow, winding mud paths, I had noticed that the open sewers, which ran along either side of me, were blocked with used food cartons, tins, rotting vegetables and excreta. I'd tried desperately to block out the stench by closing my nose and breathing only through my mouth in a poor attempt to stop myself from retching.

We had followed the narrow path as it wound its way up the mountainside passing by other huts made out of sticks and red earth. Children had been running around barefoot, dressed in old tattered dresses and shorts. I'd noticed two little girls had used large blue and red clothes-pegs as earrings, much to their amusement. All at once they stopped playing and had fallen quiet as they clustered together giggling shyly at the tall, fair-skinned, blue-eyed foreigner. I had smiled back at their beautiful brown-eyed, black- and brown-skinned faces. They'd started to follow me, curiously.

As we had approached Rose's hut, washing was hanging out on the line to dry in the heat. A pig snorted and grunted at us as it scuttled off into the grassy bank. Everything had seemed so normal with no sign of danger.

Rose had called for us to enter. The door was already open, allowing what breeze there was in, bringing some relief from the hot stifling air inside the wrought-iron hut. Nilton had gone out for the afternoon, Rose hadn't known where. She'd lifted her small frame stiffly from the bed to offer us the only seating space available. Her legs had become more infected and the pus had hardened, making it difficult for her to move around.

We'd persuaded her to remain seated on the bed, as I'd cleaned her poor legs. A big white smile had suddenly filled her shy black face; she was obviously grateful for our company. Then on Rose's request Andre and I began to pray for her and her baby.

It was then that we had heard the first shot . . .

The shooting was deafening now.

We could hear the thudding of running footsteps above our heads. The gang from Casa Branca had clearly positioned themselves just above us on the grassy slope which stretched from the hut up towards their favela on the other side of the mountain.

'A bullet came through the roof this morning,' exclaimed Rose with fear in her voice. I knew that if a bullet came through the roof now, one of us would die. Four adults covered the entire floor space of the hut.

All at once we heard the thudding of running footsteps approaching the hut. I heard myself gasp as the door flew open.

It was Claudio from our team who had been visiting another family near by. We all breathed a sigh of relief, although my heart was beating so violently I was sure everyone else could hear it.

'The shooting started as I was on my way back to our house,' Claudio said breathlessly, his eyes wide like a terrified rabbit. 'I started to run for cover, and saw this hut. This area is surrounded by bandidos. I nearly collided with one who had a machinegun. He must be up above us now on the grass bank.'

Suddenly a paralysing sensation ran through my body like a bolt of lightning. I was gripped powerfully by a fear, completely foreign to me. Panic. I started to panic inside, my emotions were in turmoil stimulated by one thought: Death ... Death ... Death. We were all going to die. What was I doing here? I've got to get out, I've got to get out ...

Unexpectedly, the fear turned to anger. And I cried out in my thoughts: God, I can't believe that you've brought me here for this. We're all going to die.

Sobs welled up from deep within me, I felt desperate.

Then all at once, an extraordinary thing occurred. I suddenly felt a rush of peace flooding through my body

7

and I had the realisation that I would be going to a much better place, I would be with Jesus, there would be so much joy.

And I completely relaxed.

A voice was singing, '*Deus esta aqui, Alleluia, tao certo como ar que eu respiro . . .*' ('God is here, Alleluia, as certain as the air that I breathe . . .'). It was Lila. We all joined in, singing at the top of our voices, laughing with a great joy which seemed to burst out from each one of our hearts.

The sounds of the bullets whistling over us became muffled. It was as though we were in a small time capsule. Andre opened his Bible and started to read from Psalm 23, 'The Lord is my shepherd, I shall not be in want. He makes me lie down in green pastures, he leads me beside quiet waters, he restores my soul . . .'

All at once I knew we would escape unharmed. I sensed a warm presence covering me, a powerful peaceful presence in that tiny slum hut, and I knew that God was with us, protecting us.

Then, as quickly as the shooting had started, it stopped. We all lay there frozen in our horizontal positions, not wanting to move. Had it really stopped, I asked myself. My ears were ringing in the silence.

'It's over,' proclaimed Andre.

We all slowly came to our feet, our bodies aching from being in the same uncomfortable positions for so long. I looked at my watch; it must have been a good thirty minutes. Not one bullet had passed through the hut. And I couldn't deny that I had witnessed the incredible protection of God.

But that night, as I climbed into my bed, the same

foreign fear returned. As I looked through the open window into the strangely still, clear night sky, I felt terror gripping my body again. My mind became full of negative thoughts. What was I doing here? What could I do to help?

I now felt too afraid to walk out on to the streets of the favela, let alone go out and help the children who had run away from this very setting to live on the perilous main streets of the city below.

For it was for these very children that, at the age of twenty-nine, I had given up all that I'd had: my luxurious apartment in London, a top salary as a TV producer, my friends and my loving family.

How had my life changed so radically? I started to question myself. Had I made a terrible mistake in coming to Brazil? What would the future hold?

2

A Taste of Glamour

'Sarah,' said my dad, in a tone of voice that caught my attention, 'you're not the sort of girl who needs to think about marriage and settling down, the world's your oyster, get a career for yourself, travel, go for it!'

And there it was, confirmation!

I was fifteen years old at the time and I've never forgotten it. We were in our kitchen at the house I grew up in, in West Horsley, Surrey. I was sitting at the pine table with my back to the window and Dad was opening the fridge. The scene remains like a 'freeze frame' in my mind.

I'd already told Mum a few months earlier, 'Don't count on me producing grandchildren for at least another fifteen years, there's just too much to do first.' Well, wasn't that what all society was saying to my generation in the mid-seventies?

So, as the eldest of three girls, I'd carefully transferred the responsibility of settling down and producing babies to my two sisters, Vanessa and Maria. Maria, the youngest, was only nine years old at the time, but she had already set her heart on an early marriage and lots of kids. So I felt pretty confident that at least one of them would fill this role satisfactorily.

10

My parents, Colin and Julie Jarman, had married on April 4th 1959 when they were only twenty years old, having met on a blind date at the Antelope pub in west London. Vanessa and I had come along soon afterwards, with only a sixteen-month gap between us. My dad was working for the National Cash Register Company at the time, earning seven pounds ten shillings a week, and we lived in a small flat at Kenilworth Court, Putney, overlooking the River Thames. Mum was regularly seen pushing her two babies in their pram to feed the ducks with stale pieces of bread.

When I was three years old we moved out of London to the countryside. Our house, in Surrey, was called Chestnuts, because we had two very large, pink-flowering chestnut trees in our front garden.

I can vividly remember the wild Beatles parties at Chestnuts in the late sixties!

Nessie and I would sit in our nighties with legs dangling over the banisters, waiting patiently for someone to pay a visit to the downstairs loo, which was under the stairs.

'Can you turn the volume down?' I'd shout at the top of my voice to the next occupant. The word 'please' had long gone from my vocabulary by the fifth effort. We'd then return to our beds with fingers crossed. But the volume never remained lowered for long. My dad, a great twister to this day, only believed in dancing to music played at full volume.

Colin, a big man with a round, smiling face, still remains one of the best story-tellers I've ever met. I used to enjoy watching him hold his audience as they waited with baited breath for the punch line. Mum, who had heard the same stories a dozen times, always laughed until her eyes filled with water. Ask any of Dad's friends and they'd say with a smile on their faces, 'Colin Jarman, he's one of the most hospitable people I know, and still makes the best gin and tonic in town.'

Known as 'Basher Jarman' in his rugby days (he was a great head-on tackler) Dad still enjoys a day out at Twickenham. I have many fond memories of cheering on England from the grandstand as a teenager, in the freezing cold winter, clothed in our sheepskin coats, woolly hats, scarves and gloves.

Today he is managing director of the UK subsidiary of a large international computer company, a position he earned through hard toil. He is and always has been a diligent worker, placing the needs of his family first, for which I have tremendous admiration. As a result of his own ambition, he was and is a wonderful encourager to his three girls. He took great pleasure in the success Vanessa and I achieved as young athletes in local and county competition. I always knew, while shaking nervously on my starting blocks waiting for the gun to go off at the start of a 100 metre race, that Dad was at the sidelines cheering me on all the way to the finishing tape. One summer our back garden was even transformed into a mini sports arena, with a long-jump pit, high jump and mini running track.

My mum has always looked as though she was my big sister. Small, slim with a blonde bob, her energetic and youthful spirit has always flattered her with at least ten years less than her actual age. Her bright intellectual mind enabled her to go back to school in her early forties and on to university, where she qualified as a teacher. She is in every sense of the word the heart of our family and our home was invariably a welcoming haven for all friends and visitors. Her artistic talents were always evident throughout the house, not least in the kitchen. Sunday lunch was a time shared with grandparents, other family members and good friends. We'd all enjoy a good roast with all the trimmings, invariably followed by apple crumble or a delicious, stodgy treacle sponge pudding.

As a family we would go to the local church on Christmas and Easter Days, and occasionally on Mothering Sundays, simply because it seemed the right thing to do. Church for me was always disappointing, apart from the fact that I never got the vicar's joke, which he would 'religiously' incorporate into his sermon. The old village church, however beautiful with its colourful stained-glass windows and ancient wall paintings, seemed as empty and as cold as some of its occupants.

Then, when I was twelve years old, something extraordinary happened to me, although I wasn't to understand its full effect on my life for another sixteen years.

I was playing at my friend Catherine's house after school one day when her elder sister and her friend invited us both to go to a youth meeting at the local village hall. It seemed like a pretty good idea at the time, so we went. I remember that Catherine and I made sure we sat right at the back of the hall. It was full of teenagers and we felt a little bit out of place. I don't recall everything that happened that night, but one thing that remains clear in my mind is that Catherine's sister and her friend stood up at the front and started to talk about Jesus and what a difference He had made in their lives. The thing that struck me more than anything was that they spoke of Jesus as though He was real, as though they knew Him personally.

And they seemed so happy and content. I was envious of them for what they had apparently found.

When I was lying in my bed later that night back at Chestnuts, I had an unusual desire to speak to this Jesus whom I'd just heard about in a way I'd never heard before.

'Jesus,' I said out loud into the stillness of the night, 'I don't know who You are, but I want to have what those girls have.' Satisfied, then, with my awkward attempt at speaking to an invisible Jesus, I went to sleep.

Suddenly, later into the night, I was woken up by what seemed to be a bright light in my room. My whole body was full of a warming heat, and I just knew that this Jesus was with me in the room. I felt no fear, only an awesome sense that He was there.

The next day I decided that I had imagined the whole experience and felt a fool to even try and explain it to anyone in my family, let alone Catherine.

But it was this very experience that was to bring me the encouragement I desperately needed, sixteen years on, when I gave up my job, family, home and friends to go to Brazil and work with the street children.

I went to a girls' day-school called Manor House, in Little Bookham, where my preference was sport: athletics, hockey, tennis, swimming. Athletics came to a standstill at the age of fifteen when I discovered boys. Training twice a week after school in the cold winter evenings at Epsom and Ewell running track soon lost its attraction after I'd found my first boyfriend. I looked older than my actual age at the time, being tall at five foot nine, and well developed!

My poor mum was forced to drive around, often at midnight, picking me up from discos and parties. And my home, with such a hospitable dad, soon attracted many a friend at weekends. It was a common sight for the neighbours of Chestnuts to see our drive full of motorbikes of all shapes and sizes. The only resistance in my household to this regular invasion came from our dog, Carlos, a springer spaniel who always chose his victims with great care. Just when the young man thought he'd won Carlos over, the dog, wagging his tail and grinning at the same time, would dig his teeth into the young man's leg with great determination. Inevitably, my mum would spend most Sunday afternoons in her bathroom attending to the wounded leg and trying to calm the sorrowful victim.

Hence, at the age of sixteen it was decided that unless I became a weekly boarder at Manor House School, I would never pass my impending O levels. It was, so my parents concluded, the only way they could 'slow me down'. The school had made me House Captain, much to a few people's surprise, but I took on the responsibility wholeheartedly and it was to be my first experience in leadership. Boarding worked, and I left with seven O levels.

Itching to get out into the big wide world, I eventually decided to do History and Art A level in one year at the technical college in Guildford. I managed to scrape by in Art only.

From the age of six I'd always said I wanted to be a nurse, so it seemed the logical thing to apply to various hospitals in London. My second interview, at the new and modern St Thomas's, was a disaster. The interviewer announced at the beginning that she was going to describe 'the worst day in the life of a nurse'. By the end of her five-minute spiel the smile on my face had turned downwards and I had to swallow a few times to get rid of the lump which had formed in my throat. The thought of dropping blood tests, toilet pans and losing three patients, all in the same night at the beginning of a week of night shifts, made me realise that I couldn't do it, I simply couldn't be a nurse after all.

My father understood me very well: he suggested I should go into something more glamorous, the media for instance! So after a year's secretarial course at the Oxford and County College in Oxford, where the principal at the time complained that I had too many boyfriends meeting me at the front entrance to the college and could bring the place a bad name, I began my search in London for an opening into the world of the media. According to my shorthand teacher, I should have applied to Buckingham Palace as a possible secretary to the Prince of Wales! I don't know who was more amused, me or my classmates. Apart from the fact that I was totally unsuitable, my shorthand was self-devised and to this day it is illegible.

Needless to say, I was probably one of the worst secretaries in the London work-place. My first job, at the age of nineteen, was as assistant secretary to Julian Senior, Vice-President of Advertising and Publicity for Warner Brothers, in the famous Wardour Street, London W1. I was soon to discover that four secretaries had either left or been sacked that month. And during my first week I was nearly the fifth.

Julian Senior, a brilliant advertiser and publicist, suffered no fool gladly. Within an hour he had taught me something I would never forget in my future career.

'Sarah,' he barked, 'trust no one and always double check!'

His number one secretary worked at 100 m.p.h. and was up from her desk and in his huge office within seconds of his first yell for her attention. In fact it seemed that everyone who worked under Julian ran and never walked.

I remember feeling totally daunted. On every wall I was surrounded by posters of newly released and up-coming movies: *Kramer vs. Kramer* with Dustin Hoffman and Meryl Streep, *Private Benjamin* with Goldie Hawn, and the famous half-nude poster of the newly discovered and stunning Bo Derek in *10*, starring with the then sex symbol of Hollywood, the cute Dudley Moore. The debate that morning was whether Bo's boobs were real or not.

Myron Karlin, the President of Warner Brothers, was over from Hollywood for a series of big meetings that week, so everyone was extra keyed up. The other excitement of the morning was the arrival of their first fax machine, which in January 1980 was something to get excited about. It was huge in comparison to today's compact machines and took up the space of half a desktop. I tried to look as though I understood what it did as Julian's secretary attempted to explain.

Then suddenly everyone left for the meeting, leaving me alone to answer the phones and take messages. One small challenge was the intercom on my desk which was apparently used to communicate with all personnel internally. 'Should you need me urgently, dial 344,' said Julian as he walked out of the office followed by his team. No sooner had they left than in walked one of the shortest men I'd ever seen. He was smoking a fat cigar so I figured he must be important.

'Hi,' he said, 'I'm Myron Karlin. Where's Julian?' Taken aback, I explained that he'd just missed him. Myron left the office, leaving behind him a waft of cigar smoke. A few minutes later the intercom buzzed. It was Julian.

'Anything up?' barked Julian.

'Yes,' I replied, loudly so as to make sure he could hear me. 'Um, um . . .' I'd forgotten my recent visitor's name. Julian was getting impatient.

'The President was here,' I tried.

'Who?' barked Julian.

'You know, the short little fat man,' I said desperately. I'd had enough.

There was deathly silence. Oh dear, I thought, a sense of humour failure. But it was worse. Myron Karlin had been in the room with Julian the whole time. The intercom clicked dead, and I was sure that in a few minutes I would too.

Julian wasn't pleased. But water was soon thrown on the fire because Myron thought it was the funniest thing he'd heard for ages; in fact from then on he signed his article in the monthly international newsletters '. . . from the short little fat man'! I thanked God for the President's sense of humour.

During my year at Warner Brothers I tasted glamour for the first time, not least when I was sent to Los Angeles as a courier with a copy of Stanley Kubrick's film *The Shining*, starring Jack Nicholson, for a private screening in Hollywood.

Apart from the fact that I was scared out of my wits and didn't sleep a wink after seeing the film, I did enjoy my free bottle of champagne which came with compliments from the manager of the Beverly Wilshire Hotel, where I was staying. And I do remember lying in the bath in the luxurious hotel bathroom, talking to Mum on the phone while sipping a glass of the bubbly stuff and thinking, this is the life!

And so it was that at the age of twenty I broke off a two-year relationship with my boyfriend and flew off to California. My first year was spent travelling and partying. Needless to say I fell in love once again, this time with a handsome young executive from the Walt Disney Studios. We set up home in a small beach house on Ninth Place and Ocean Drive in Manhattan Beach, just outside Los Angeles. I became completely caught up in the beach scene of 'the body beautiful' and before long I was a near anorexic, eating cottage cheese and pineapple all day and jogging non-stop with the other fanatics on a special path for joggers only, which ran along the coast for miles. Most of the beach crowd were taking drugs of all types. But a good friend of mine had once said to me, 'Sarah, don't try cocaine, I know you and you'll love it and want more.' Somehow those words always rang like a warning bell every time I was tempted. Looking back I can see it was God's protection.

Evette, my best friend at the advertising agency where I worked in downtown LA, was a Christian. She never made me feel guilty for the way I was living and she never preached at me. But I saw in the way Evette lived out her life that she was different to most other girls my age. She had a profound peace in all she did. I only went once with Evette to her church and I remember absolutely nothing except the overwhelming love the people seemed to have for one another.

After two and a half years in Los Angeles I became restless once again. I still felt too young and unpeaceful to marry. There just seemed a lot more to do first. So finishing another relationship I went back to London.

At twenty-two I was ready for a career challenge. And after eighty letters, fifteen interviews and three months of toil, I eventually landed the job I'd only ever dreamed about. Dennis Davidson Associates, a major international entertainment public relations agency, offered me a month's trial as head of the Provincial Publicity Department, promoting feature films in production and distribution outside London. The starting salary was a pittance at £4,600 per annum, but that wasn't a priority at the time.

The first film I worked on was *Superman III* starring Christopher Reeve, Richard Pryor, the outrageous Pamela Stephenson and the talented Gene Hackman. We organised a meal at the famous Kettner's Restaurant in the West End, to which key provincial press and radio were invited from all over the UK to have lunch with Christopher Reeve, Pamela Stephenson, the Salkind brothers, producers of all the Superman movies, and the director, Richard Lester.

After the Royal Premier, held in Leicester Square, there was a lavish party at a nearby hotel attended by the rich and famous, and the not so famous. Money was not spared. In fact it was never spared on most of the large movies. Publicity and advertising were essential if there was going to be a good opening. However, after the first two to three weeks of the release of a movie, high audience figures depended primarily on word of mouth. If the film wasn't liked no amount of advertising and publicity could convince the public otherwise. But *Superman III* was a success and got loads of press write-ups and radio and television coverage around the United Kingdom. And I passed my month's trial with a very encouraging hand-written note from Dennis Davidson himself. The Provincial Publicity Department consisting only of me and one other was soon to treble in size.

The challenge for any publicist was getting publicity for an unknown actor or actress, a new producer and director or a small film. One of my most enjoyable campaigns was for a Hugh Hudson (director of *Chariots of Fire*) film called *Greystoke, the Legend of Tarzan*, which starred the then unknown Frenchman, Christopher Lambert. He had spent six months living with real gorillas and chimpanzees in preparation for the movie, and could speak 'monkey language' both verbally and physically so convincingly that I often became quite unnerved and would have to remind myself that he was a human being after all.

Hugh Hudson wanted a large provincial campaign which included two weeks of travelling around Scotland and Birmingham, Manchester and other cities doing radio, television and press interviews. As a publicist your worst enemy was the transport. You depended completely on flights and trains leaving on time and traffic being as clear as possible in order to meet your pre-planned schedule. When transport failed you, you quickly had to play piggy-in-the-middle, keeping the actors, directors and producers calm and happy, explaining to the respective media why you were running late, which wasn't always easy if the show was live, and finally you had to keep yourself as cool as possible to avoid becoming a nail-biting, gibbering idiot. It was an art that could only be learned through each unfortunate experience.

The two weeks with Hugh Hudson and Christopher Lambert were exhausting but a lot of fun. And although on a number of occasions they had to walk into live shows at the last minute due to traffic jams, rail strikes and delayed flights, I managed to come back to London with a few unbitten nails. However, I will never forget the faces of some of the employees from Marks & Spencer in Manchester as Christopher Lambert did his gorilla act outside their main entrance so convincingly that they didn't know whether to laugh or call the police.

The famous Cannes Film Festival in the south of France was a must if you had anything to do with the business. Dennis Davidson took out a large team every year to co-ordinate most of the publicity for most of the movies being sold to possible international distributors, not forgetting the films in the various competitions held to discover the best movie, actor, actress, producer, director, newcomer and so on. Cannes was and still is a colourful collage of the famous, the would-be famous, the outrageous, the hangers-on, the distributors, producers, directors, publicists, actors, media and of course the paparazzi. Restaurants along the well-known beachfront promenade would hire out large tables on the sand at lunch-times where people could rub shoulders sipping chilled rosé wine, spotting anyone familiar and admiring the semi-nude or nude girls desperate to attract the lenses of the paparazzi.

I had the privilege of meeting and working with many talented artists and film makers. But my favourite film was *The Killing Fields*, produced by David Puttnam and directed by Roland Joffe (*The Mission*). The film was based on a true story which Puttnam claimed to have read in a small column of the *New York Times Magazine* while on the loo in his house one weekend. The story told of an incredible friendship between Sydney Schanberg, the war correspondent of the *New York Times*, and his assistant, Dith Pran, a courageous Cambodian-born man, during Cambodia's revolutionary Khmer Rouge war against the Lon Nol government which started in 1975. The film was an all-round masterpiece, from the script to the sensitive acting of Sam Waterston and Dr Haing S. Ngor, an actual evacuee from the war itself. When I finished promoting *The Killing Fields* in early 1985, I remember saying to my mum, 'Well, that's it for me. I might as well change jobs because I will never work on any film as fulfilling as this one.'

And so it was that a year later I left Dennis Davidson Associates to go into the world of television production. Michael Hurll, Executive Producer for Light Entertainment Programmes for the BBC, was looking for researchers for one of his most successful productions at the time, *The Late Late Breakfast Show*.

On my first day at the BBC Television Centre in Shepherd's Bush, London, I was sent to do the rounds of the party political conferences in Blackpool and Harrogate with a camera crew to interview the politicians. No, nothing serious, only silliness. Questions like, 'What is your favourite fish?' and 'Do you know what a crustacean is?' and 'Can you spell it?'

Amazingly, they were all only too delighted to answer these questions. Was it a refreshing break from discussing how they could better life in the United Kingdom, I asked myself. But no, they were all excellent actors and actresses,

23

fully aware of the fact that *The Late Late Breakfast Show* had the highest viewing figures of any light entertainment show at peak time on Saturday afternoons.

My favourite answer to 'Do you know what a crustacean is?' came from Dr David Owen, who replied, 'Which station?' When I repeated the question he responded with satisfaction, 'St Pancras Station!' (A crustacean, by the way, is an aquatic animal with jointed legs and a hard shell.)

But I was caught out myself when Tom King MP asked me, 'Can *you* spell it?' And I have to admit that, put on the spot, I couldn't, much to my crew's amusement. That bit was cut out in the editing suite!

For Christmas Day in 1986 we produced a live, two-hour show linking up major cities throughout the UK with Sydney, Melbourne and Perth in Australia. The main theme was to reunite relatives. I was sent to Sydney with a lady who was to be reunited with her mother on the show after twenty years. Her two young children came with her and I was asked to make a small film of their journey. On our way to Australia we stopped in Singapore where a schedule had been organised for us by a local television station, and for forty-eight hours we never stopped, visiting stunning orchid fields, riding through the old part of the city in rickshaw bicycles, seeing the Christmas lights, receiving a present from Father Christmas. However, it was our visit to the zoo which was the most challenging for us all. We had a pre-arranged appointment to have breakfast with an orang-utan. I don't know who was more afraid, us, the film crew or the ape. He was huge and insisted on a food fight at eight o'clock in the morning. But our Singapore guides assured us that this breakfast experience was a great privilege as there was a considerable waiting list. It was hard to smile and look grateful.

From Sydney I flew on to Melbourne where I was to co-ordinate a live link-up between the English cricket team and their families – those who were unable to join them – in the UK. It was the night before the start of the final Test and the manager was rightly concerned about them getting an early night. Unfortunately Christmas morning in the UK is Christmas evening in Australia, so an early night was not had, which gave the hungry press something to write about. However, it apparently didn't affect their play as England won the Test, captained by Mike Gatting.

In December 1983 I had started another relationship with a then sub-editor for BBC TV News. In the three years that we went out together he was successfully promoted to general reporter, occasional presenter and eventually to sports correspondent and presenter for the BBC before being won over to ITN as, initially, their sports man. But the more successful our two careers became, the worse our relationship grew. When I wasn't working he was, and vice versa. By the end of 1986 our relationship was in crisis. There was no fear of God and therefore no faithfulness and loyalty to one another. Needless to say we started to destroy each other emotionally, which is one of the most terrible things that can happen between two people. I fell into a depression and can remember being totally unable to get out of bed in the mornings and sometimes not even wanting to wake up. I was exhausted and by the middle of 1987 we went our separate ways. But the emotional hurts remained and it was then that I started to question my life and what it was really all about.

During 1987 I worked on various television productions for the BBC, including *Top of the Pops*, *The BPI Awards* (major British music awards), *The BAFTA Awards* (the awards ceremony of the British Academy of Film and Television Arts), *Now For Something Else* with Rory Bremner, *Summertime Special* (a series of six one-hour shows, all shot on location in Jersey) and *Whatever Next?* with Noel Edmonds.

In November of that same year, my cousin Fiona insisted that I go to church with her in London. I resisted for as long as possible, until eventually I ran out of excuses. I had been a couple of times with her in the past, but apart from the enjoyable songs and music the whole evening had washed over me like water off a duck's back. However, on this particular winter's evening as I entered the doors of Holy Trinity Brompton with Fiona I knew it was going to be different. The large church, situated behind the Brompton Oratory, seats over one thousand people and I made sure I was right at the back in the upstairs gallery. It was a nice safe distance from the front and easy to make a getaway if need be. But that night I couldn't help but notice all the hundreds and hundreds of young, normal-looking people, flooding into the church and seeming as though they really wanted to be there. They were smiling and laughing and there was an air of excitement.

The time of worship at the beginning of the service began. There was a live band and the songs had simple words that the people around me appeared to sing as though they personally knew the person they were meant for . . .

Such love, pure as the whitest snow,
Such love weeps for the shame I know,
Such love, paying the debt I owe,
O Jesus, such love.

As I joined in I became aware of how much I hungered for this love.

Such love, stilling my restlessness,
Such love, filling my emptiness,
Such love, showing me holiness,
O Jesus, such love.

Suddenly it was as though my whole body became flooded with a warm heat, a heat that seemed to wash through me from my head to my feet over and over again. And I knew I had been touched by God. I knew instantly that Jesus was real. I knew that this was what I had been searching for all these years. We sang on.

Such love springs from eternity,
Such love, pouring through history,
Such love, fountain of life to me,
O Jesus, such love,
O Jesus, such love.

I sat down and wept and wept. They weren't tears of sadness, they were tears of relief, of joy, of repentance. That night when Nicky Gumbel, the curate, stood up at the front of the church in a casual jumper and trousers, and spoke so humbly and simply about Jesus Christ, the Son of God, who had died for us, in our place, that our sins might be forgiven, that we might be reunited with our Father in heaven, the creator of all life, I knew it was the truth. It was as though his every word cut through into my heart.

3

Hollywood or Brazil?
My Will or Yours?

'Flight number QS10 to Sydney is boarding now from gate 4, final call.' The announcement rang out for the second time in the international departure area of Terminal 3 at Heathrow Airport.

It was December 23rd 1987 and I was on my way to Australia once again for BBC's *A Christmas Morning/Evening with Noel Edmonds*. This time the three-hour live show would link up five countries around the world, thanks to the incredible technology of telecommunications and satellites. With me were a selection of people who would be reunited with their long-lost relatives in Australia. Two brothers, who had been separated when they were two and four years old, would finally meet after forty years. Their single mother, unable to support two children, had sent the elder brother to Australia with the Salvation Army to be adopted. I will never forget when they embraced each other during the show on Christmas evening, in a crowded harbour-side pub in Sydney. Two very big, broad men, so alike and, as they were to find out, with so much in common; their two daughters had the same names, they were both avid fishermen.

I cannot tell you at exactly what point during the three-hour live show I knew I was not going back to England,

29

but my mind was made up by the early hours of Boxing Day morning as I climbed into bed, exhausted, in my hotel room.

My contract for the show was up. And although I did have a return ticket it was valid for one year. Michael Hurll from the BBC, although a little surprised by my decision, wished me well, as did my parents. And so it was that I worked for a year in Sydney for Village Roadshow Corporation, film producers and distributors, as a publicist once again.

The greatest fun I had that year was promoting the re-release of that famous children's movie, Walt Disney's *101 Dalmatians*. Hiring out the impressive front steps of the famous Sydney Opera House with the spectacular view of the harbour behind it, I arranged through the Dalmatian Club for 101 real Dalmatian dogs to meet for an hour at lunch-time a week before the film was released. A great friend, who was tall and skinny enough, gave a very convincing appearance as the wicked Cruella. All the dog owners took their parts very seriously and dressed in black and white polka dots. Even the cast on a broken leg of one of the owners was covered in black spots! Every national TV station and newspaper photographer turned up for the photocall. It was chaos. Someone even tried counting the number of dogs but gave up, complaining of a headache.

The problem was that a group of Greek dancers were to dance on the very same steps that afternoon as part of some special Greek celebration. And so we had been firmly instructed by the manager of the Sydney Opera House, 'On no account are you to leave behind one single dog turd!'

This order was taken very seriously by all the Dalmatian

owners, who were seen, plastic bags in hand, picking up their dogs' doings with the utmost dedication.

But it was all very worth while and a sight not easily forgotten. We even made news headlines in Hollywood, appearing in the *Los Angeles Times*.

I found a small church in Paddington, where I was living, not far from downtown Sydney. The pastor, an elderly man, took me under his wing and would meet me once a week at lunch-times to answer my many questions: How did we know the validity of the Bible? Was everything in it the truth? Why and how should I read the Bible? How can I be sure of my faith? Does God really have a plan for each one of our lives? How do we hear God's voice? And on and on went my questions. Patiently and with much knowledge and wisdom he would answer them one by one.

But I was still resisting, and although I couldn't deny the experiences I'd had with God, it was a slow process.

By the end of 1988 and at the age of twenty-eight, I flew back to England for Christmas on my way to Africa, where I was going to co-produce a series of six TV adventure documentaries called *Journey through Africa*, presented by a 'living Aussie Tarzan' called Michael Calnan. Channel 10 in Australia had committed themselves to paying 50 per cent of the budget, and we had a meeting with Channel 4 in London to confirm their commitment to the other 50 per cent.

While I was in England, however, all my plans were to be turned upside down.

The Sunday before Christmas 1988 I woke up with an overwhelming desire to go to Holy Trinity Brompton. And so that evening, alone, I walked through the doors of the crowded old church and made sure I was sitting right at the back.

Once again, taken unawares, I wept throughout the entire service feeling that same powerful presence of God upon me. At the end of the service the vicar, Sandy Millar, said that there was someone in the congregation to whom God was saying, 'Walk My way, not yours.' As soon as he spoke, it was as though a spotlight had been turned on above me. I knew it was me. Unable to remain seated I stood up, in fact I almost felt myself being lifted up. When Sandy Millar prayed, I couldn't hear a word he said, but inside my own thoughts I heard the following words, 'Don't go to Africa now, for when you go you will go for Me. Stay in England. Do a course with this church. Don't go back to Australia.' I sat down feeling weak and confused.

That evening, smoking a cigarette, I talked things through with my cousin Fiona in a nearby restaurant. It couldn't be true; surely I hadn't heard God's voice, and least of all telling me to give up all my previously made plans. It was impossible. But Fiona eventually said, 'Sarah, it is your life, it is your decision. Either you listen and obey God now, or you put all His plans for you on hold for yet another year.'

So there and then in the restaurant I pathetically and half-heartedly said to an invisible God that if it really was Him, He would have to make it impossible for me to leave England. And by Christmas Eve, a week later, that was exactly what happened.

Channel 4 called me up with numerous apologies saying that they had had a meeting and changed their minds about financing *Journey through Africa*. They were already investing in a similar documentary and thought our series too much like the other. Then the second blow came soon after from the Australian Embassy: they had decided not to renew my visa to re-enter their country. And so there it was, confirmation.

I soon discovered that Holy Trinity Brompton were about to run a relatively new course starting in January for three months on Wednesday nights, called the Alpha Course. The course was to cover the basic beliefs of the Christian faith.

At the same time Michael Hurll from the BBC, who had started his own television production company in the West End, offered me work as co-producer on a new five-night-a-week chat show for Rupert Murdoch's latest enterprise, Sky Satellite Television, which had just been launched. The show, presented by Derek Jameson, was to be called *Jameson Tonight*. I was attracted to the challenge of starting up a brand new show. Also the salary was excellent at £1000 a week.

The old Windmill Theatre off Shaftesbury Avenue was chosen as the venue for *Jameson Tonight* and work started immediately on putting in the set, the studio lighting, a recording suite for the director and his team, the cables for the cameras, an editing suite and changing rooms for the artists. Meanwhile I set about interviewing national newspaper journalists for possible researchers, and looking for a band that would be a regular feature on the show. The format was to be a magazine news chat show, with up-to-date headlines, people in the news, politicians, eccentrics, Joe Public, pop stars, comedians, movie stars and so on. The young and pretty Annabel Giles was chosen as Derek's sidekick. Our offices were just around the corner from the theatre on Brewer Street, off Berwick Street market. By April 1989 we were recording our first show.

At night after the show, as I left for home from the old Windmill Theatre, I started to notice young boys and girls sleeping out on the streets around Piccadilly. I would stop to talk to some of them and most had the same story. They'd come from Scotland, Wales or the north of England to London looking for a better life. Their parents had split up and one or the other was now an alcoholic and couldn't support them. The kids and teenagers I met were miserable and lost. Without a permanent address they couldn't get work and without work they couldn't get an address. I became outraged that in a first world country there should be kids and teenagers sleeping on the streets.

Then I discovered a new night shelter off Shaftesbury Avenue, run and supported by the local council, where a few kids and teenagers could find a bed at night as well as help from an on-staff social worker. A friend told me that they were looking for volunteers to cook and serve dinner and spend the night in the Centre with the kids. As I was working just around the corner I offered to do this one night a week.

I will never forget the anger that those young homeless had. One tall, lanky teenager stands out in my mind. He would wear a t-shirt with a design he had drawn of Satan on the front. He refused to take it off or to wash it in case the drawing disappeared. One morning at breakfast I asked him, 'How do you know that Satan looks like your drawing?'

He looked back at me through his cold grey eyes and answered, 'I see him at night in my dreams. He talks to me and tells me that my life isn't worth living.'

I was shocked by his frankness. Also at the thought that Satan was so real. Trying to pull myself together, I asked, 'Do you know what Jesus looks like? Because He can give you a new life that is worth living.'

'Yeah, I know, but I'm not interested in changing my t-shirt,' he answered nonchalantly. I felt frustrated, knowing that only Jesus could give him the new life he so desperately needed.

The thirteen months producing *Jameson Tonight* were exhausting and there was little time for a social life. I was making a huge salary, yet somehow it all seemed to disappear with little to show for it. Efforts to get thin by joining an expensive exercise club in Piccadilly achieved little, as the battle with my weight continued. Meanwhile, although I had the job that I'd always wanted to do, my priorities were changing. One weekend when I was praying with friends, God gave me a verse that changed my life from that moment on: 'Be still, and know that I am God' (Psalm 46:10a). I knew instantly that I had to let go of my future. I had to stop making my own plans, stop restlessly looking ahead. I had to be still and live one day at a time, trusting God to take care of my agenda. And instantly I was filled with a deep peace that I had never felt before in my whole life.

On a winter's evening one Sunday in January 1990, sitting in church I asked God what He wanted me to do for Him. Suddenly, as clearly as I'd heard Him telling me in December 1988 not to go to Africa or to return to Australia but to stay in England, I heard in my thoughts, 'I want you to go to Brazil.'

I was stunned. Was that me or was that God? Brazil? I'd

never planned to go to Brazil . . . my mind became full of questions . . . What goes on there? Why Brazil? Surely God wanted me to stay working in television in London?

Unknown to me, Loren Cunningham, founder of the international and interdenominational organisation Youth With A Mission, was the guest speaker that night. At the end of his challenging talk on the mission field he asked all those in the congregation who wanted 'to go' for Christ to stand up and he'd pray for them. Once again I felt a spotlight come on over me, and I stood up nervously to give my life over to go wherever God wanted me to be.

As I was leaving the church that night a friend came up to me and said, 'You know, Sarah, when God tells you the country He wants you to go to you cannot say no.' Today my friend cannot remember saying these words to me but I have never forgotten. In fact I felt shocked at the time, thinking that it couldn't be all that clear cut.

In early June, after I'd finished my thirteen-month contract with *Jameson Tonight*, I went to Israel for two weeks. Although two thousand years on, it was a privilege to be able to see with my own eyes the places where Jesus Himself had walked: the Sea of Galilee, Capernaum, Jerusalem, Bethlehem, the Mount of Olives. But it was when we were in the Garden of Gethsemane, where Jesus Himself, before He was about to be arrested and crucified on the cross, had said to God, 'Abba, Father, everything is possible for you. Take this cup from me. Yet not what I will, but what you will' (Mark 14:36), that I was most overawed. I sat down with this amazing realisation of what Jesus had done for me and I wept. There and then I prayed, 'My Father in heaven, not as I will, but as You will.'

When I eventually stood up I discovered that the group I was with had been patiently waiting for me for over half an hour. But I knew that something had happened within me and that there was no going back.

From the minute I got home to London it was as though every magazine and newspaper I read had an article about Rio de Janeiro. Every time I turned on the TV or radio there was a report on Rio de Janeiro. I even got a postcard sent to me with a picture of the famous Christ Redeemer statue in Rio. It became a joke.

Finally, in early August on a teaching weekend run by Nicky Gumbel, I met a young woman called Lydia from Peru through whom God was going to clarify everything. She had come to England aged twenty with a one-way ticket and no visa. Her family were very poor but faithful Christians, and she had received a prophecy on her twentieth birthday that God had called her to England. Impossible as it seemed to her and her family, they trusted God to provide everything she would need. Sure enough she received enough money to buy a flight to London. But she had no visa, and this was the final test she put to God. If it really was His will He'd have to take care of it. When she arrived at Heathrow Airport she told the truth, through a translator, to the immigration officers who had pulled her aside. They asked her to wait in a small room. After some hours they returned, saying she could stay.

When I met her, Lydia had already been in London for some years and spoke excellent English. She was currently working in the Well Coffee Shop run by St Michael's Church, opposite Victoria Station. There she had an office with a window overlooking the inside of the shop. God would tell her who to go and speak to and she would come out of her office and go to join that particular person at his or her table. Inevitably that person was in a lot of trouble, very sad, even considering suicide. In just the previous year over four hundred people had asked Jesus into their lives through this small Peruvian missionary.

I knew after hearing her testimony that I had to talk to her.

First Lydia just wanted to listen to my story. And eventually I confessed to her all my doubts: leaving my family, my career, my friends, my apartment. And even more important, at the age of twenty-nine I wanted to get married and to have children soon which, I'd convinced myself, couldn't happen if I left everything and became a missionary in Brazil.

'Sarah,' she said with a sigh, 'you are listening to the old lie, from the old liar.'

'What do you mean?' I asked, intrigued.

'Satan does not want you to go, because he knows that God has important plans for you. So he is telling you the one thing that you do not want to hear, because this will distract you from trusting in God and obeying Him.'

I was speechless.

Lydia then prayed for me, rebuking the lies and all the doubts I had in the name of Jesus Christ. The minute she did this I felt a huge weight go off my shoulders and I started to weep, as once again God's warm presence flooded my body. Suddenly Lydia stopped praying and she said, 'God has given me two verses for you. The first is in relation to your desire to get married. Psalm 37, verses 4 to 6: "Delight yourself in the Lord and he will give you the desires of your heart. Commit your way to the Lord; trust in him and he will do this: He will make your righteousness shine like the dawn, the justice of your cause like the noonday sun." Sarah, delight yourself in the Lord, and He'll take care of the rest. Not the other way around. He is all you need.'

She went on, 'The second verse I have for you is from Jeremiah, chapter 33, verse 3: "Call to me and I will answer you and tell you great and unsearchable things you do not know." Sarah, God wants to speak to you.'

That evening we prayed once again together. Only this time it was me who did the talking.

'Lord tell me what you want me to do for you in Brazil,' I asked expectantly. We waited for an answer.

Eventually Lydia said to me, 'When you ask something from God He always answers. But sometimes you have to be patient. Even if it takes all night we will wait.'

I asked again for a second time. And we waited. Then a third time.

Suddenly, as quick as a flash, I saw a picture in my mind. It was of the Pied Piper, dancing on the streets playing his musical pipe, and all these dirty little street urchins were dancing behind him, laughing and singing.

I prayed out loud, 'God, what does it mean?'

Then as clear as can be I heard in my thoughts, 'You are a Pied Piper, Sarah, and you are dancing these children out of danger.'

I was completely confused and shared what I'd seen and heard with Lydia. My mind became full of questions: Who are these children? I've never worked with children in my life! I can't play a musical instrument! Then once again I heard in my thoughts God's calm voice, 'Sarah, it's My love that will draw the children to you, not a musical instrument.'

At that time Amnesty International had not released their horrifying reports about the street children and their deaths at the hands of the extermination squads. There had been no major publicity in the media.

But the next day I was to find out. Lynne Green, a director at Youth With A Mission, came to speak to us about their work and training schools. At the end of his talk I asked him if he knew Brazil.

'Yes,' he said with a smile. 'As a matter of fact I've just come back from there.'

I couldn't believe my luck. I asked on.

'Do you know if there are children on the streets who are in danger?'

'Danger?' he said with concern in his voice. 'There are millions of children forced to live on the streets because of terrible home situations, and hundreds are being murdered.'

The minute I heard those words I knew I couldn't stay. If God could save some of those children through my life I had a responsibility to obey, even if I couldn't understand how.

I started to pray regularly for the children and for God to show me clearly what I was to do next. But I wouldn't have to wait long to find out.

It seemed that everyone I spoke to suggested the same thing. 'Why don't you do a discipleship training school with Youth With A Mission? Their first ever base in Lausanne, Switzerland, is supposed to have excellent teaching.'

Aware that I needed more preparation, and that I would not be wise to simply pack up my bags and fly to Rio de Janeiro alone, I telephoned the base in Lausanne.

I was quickly informed that they had a school for five months starting in three weeks at the end of September, and that for the first time they would be sending the team to Chile, in South America, for two months' practical work. There were still places available and it would all cost around £2000. I thanked them very much, explaining that I was on my way to Brazil and not to Chile.

But later that night while saying a quick prayer I heard that same calm voice in my thoughts, 'Sarah, Chile will be a stepping-stone to Brazil. I want you to do the school in Lausanne.' I couldn't believe it. Surely, I thought, not Chile? Where on earth would I get £2000? Why hadn't God told me all this in June? I'd spent most of my savings in my three-month break since finishing *Jameson Tonight*.

The following day my grandmother, a Christian, asked me out of the blue what my plans were. Taken aback I explained to her, as best I could, what I believed God wanted me to do.

'Well,' she asked, 'how much will you need?'

'I need £2000,' I replied.

'Um,' she pondered. 'Well, I can give it to you now, or you can have it when I die. If you need it now then that makes more sense.'

It was all happening so fast. But I thanked God and my grandmother and kept going forward, sending off my application form to Youth With A Mission in Switzerland. My pastor, Nicky Gumbel, and his family gave their blessings. My mother, who had become a Christian around the same time as me, gave hers. My father, who wasn't yet a Christian, found it hard to understand everything that had happened to his successful eldest daughter. But, wanting to see me happy, he put his own doubts aside and

wished me all the very best. My two sisters, Vanessa and
Maria, were behind me as ever. Maria was already married
with a son, Jack, my parents' first grandchild.

Then, all at once, I started to get job offers to work on
highly successful television programmes. I couldn't believe
it. But every time I thought about throwing in the idea of
going to Switzerland and taking one of the offers, all the
peace I had left me and I felt restless and insecure. There
was simply no going back.

I was on my way to Brazil.

42

4

The Devil's Playground

'We will be arriving in Rio de Janeiro an hour from now. Why don't you try and get some sleep?' said Lennart with a strong Spanish accent. We'd been travelling together by bus for three days from Santiago, Chile, through Argentina and now Brazil. However tired I was I couldn't sleep. The excitement was too much. Here I was, finally in Brazil; it was March 29th 1991.

The hilly countryside around us was full of tropical plants and trees in all shades of rich greens, and the exotic flowers stood out in their bright reds, purples, mauves, oranges and yellows. Alongside the narrow road we were travelling meandered a fast-flowing river, and cattle were grazing up the grassy banks beyond it in the warmth of the early morning sun. Charming old farmhouses painted white were dotted around the hills. Argentina had been so flat and dry in comparison.

'O Lord,' I said under my breath, 'I'm finally here. What lies ahead, only You know. This time You are the producer, the writer and the director. The script is in Your hand.'

I was on my way, via Rio de Janeiro, to Belo Horizonte, the third largest city in Brazil, to do a 'Rescue and Restoration' course for three months with a Dutch couple,

43

Johan and Jeanette Lukasse. They had worked with street children for five years and ran a Rescue and Restoration house in the city centre. I'd heard about the course through a Brazilian missionary who had come to Lausanne for a couple of months while I was there. After the course I would be returning to Rio de Janeiro.

As I looked out of the window, I started to reflect on my past five months in Switzerland and Chile which seemed to have passed so quickly. My first few days in Switzerland had been very difficult and I had questioned God on a number of occasions as to whether it really was His will that I was there. One morning some verses had popped into my mind out of the blue. And I had quickly opened my Bible to read with astonishment the following: 'to prepare God's people for works of service, so that the body of Christ may be built up until we all reach unity in the faith and in the knowledge of the Son of God and become mature, attaining to the whole measure of the fulness of Christ' (Eph. 4:12–13). It was spot on.

God was humbling me and I had to come face to face with my ugly pride. Suddenly I was no longer Sarah Jarman the TV producer. Instead I was quite simply Sarah Jarman the equal of everyone else in the school. Paul wrote in his letter to the Galatians: 'Am I now trying to win the approval of men or of God? Or am I trying to please men? If I were still trying to please men, I would not be a servant of Christ.' This had spoken to me so clearly. The only simile I could think of to describe how I felt was of a ripe banana being peeled of its skin, a piece at a time, until left bare with its flesh only. All the old protection, the old fronts, the supports, the titles, were being stripped away from me until I was left feeling vulnerable, a nobody.

Eventually, desperate, I said, 'Lord, I am so weak, I am nothing before You, make me into the woman You always wanted me to be. I want Your glory to shine through me, not mine.' It had become clear that nothing I was ever going to do for God would make Him love me more than He did already. What I would do for Christ would be a consequence of my own relationship with Him. Not the other way around.

One day after a service in the Lausanne base a young man from Egypt, who was doing a counselling school, came up to me and said that he'd like to share something with me. He explained that God had shown him a vision of me as a child. I was around eleven or twelve years old and I was in bed; it was the middle of the night. He said that Jesus had been standing beside my bedside looking over me. As he spoke my eyes filled with tears, and I remembered clearly that experience I'd had at twelve years old which I'd denied the next day as having been only my imagination.

'Sarah,' Nashaat said gently, 'I believe God wants you to know that He called you to serve Him from that night on, and that His hand has been upon you to this day. Don't fear the future. Trust in your heavenly Father.'

It was exactly what I needed to hear. Because I was afraid.

In Chile I had travelled south with three others from the group to the breathtaking islands off Puerto Montt where Indians still lived and survived as they had done for hundreds of years. We had been welcomed into their small simple homes as though we were from their own families and offered the food from their very own plates. To refuse would have been the biggest offence. We took water from a deep well, washed in a bucket and used a hole in the ground for our toilet. All the material luxury of the Western world had been absent, but we had all been very content and adapted without complaints. Maybe the beauty around us compensated. The islands had been covered in wild pastures full of flowers; the sea was always brimming with jumping dolphins and tuna; eagles, hawks and seagulls had spread their wings and coasted high above us in the blue skies, and snow-capped volcanic mountains were always visible on the horizon.

We had prayed and interceded for the local people. Many were sick and had sought us out for prayer. One old woman in particular had been suffering excruciating pain throughout her whole body. She had been bedridden for two months. I would never forget the pain that showed in her withered face and sunken dark eyes. We had prayed for her for over two hours, until suddenly her tiny room had been filled with the warm and powerful presence of the Lord. Her two daughters who were with us had burst into tears. Then all at once the old withered face had started to change before our own eyes, becoming fuller and pinker. The pain, so she said, had lessened considerably.

In early March we had met up with the rest of our team in Santiago, the capital of Chile, from where they had all caught a flight back to Switzerland leaving me behind, with tearful goodbyes, to make my way directly to Brazil. The money which I had needed for my journey to Belo Horizonte via Rio had arrived, out of the blue, a week before I was due to leave. A letter from my pastor, Nicky Gumbel, and his family had somehow found me safely and it included an offering for exactly the amount I would need to catch a bus from Chile through Brazil, and then a plane on to Belo Horizonte from Rio. It was an answer to prayer because no one knew what I needed. Once again I saw that God was in control of this big adventure I had embarked on.

'We're arriving at Rio's bus station,' said Lennart, bringing me back to reality.

Lennart, a young Chilean, had been the only person who spoke English on the bus. He also played the guitar brilliantly, which every passenger had enjoyed. We said goodbye to one another, as he left to stay with a friend in Rio before leaving for Germany.

'Sarah Jarman?' asked a girl from behind me. I turned around to find a short, rounded girl with a large smile and an even larger hat with bottle corks dangling from the brim.

'Hi, Sarah, I'm Myriam from the Youth With A Mission base here in Rio. I am so glad to meet you.' She gave me a big hug. 'You must be exhausted! I will be taking you to the airport. Unfortunately we have to take two buses and it's started to rain. I'm so sorry,' she said apologetically, as though it was all her fault. She spoke excellent English with no trace of a Brazilian accent.

Raining! I'd never seen a downfall like it. We eventually arrived at Ilha do Governador Airport drenched. After checking in my wet suitcases I followed her to a coffee bar where we would kill the next two hours before my flight to Belo Horizonte.

'Sarah,' she said, taking sips from her cup of the strongest and sweetest coffee I'd ever tasted, 'we are so excited that you are here, you are an answer to our prayers. And I believe God is going to do wonderful things through your life here in these children's lives. He has a specific plan for you.'

I felt overwhelmed by her openness.

'You know,' she continued, 'there are millions of children throughout this country who are abandoned, needy and walking the streets. Hundreds are being killed.' Her whole face was full of expression and her dark brown eyes were alive and full of righteous anger.

'I was horrified to read that 472 children were murdered here in Rio by the extermination squad last year, and that these guys are well paid for killing,' I said, feeling sick to my stomach. 'And apparently the squads are often made up of military and civilian policemen and private security guards.'

Myriam nodded and ordered more coffee. I declined and ordered fresh orange juice instead. My mouth was dry and my head felt dizzy, the effects of three days on a bus.

I had also read that the Government had set up a national commission, with equal numbers of representatives from government departments and non-government organisations, specifically dedicated to the defence of these children's rights. They recommended investigations of death-squad killing, a review of police recruitment and training, legal sanctions against police officers accused of using violence against children and greater control of security companies, especially those employing police officers and security guards who were shown to be members of death squads. The problem with these recommendations, however, was that police forces were controlled by the states, not the federal government. Each state had both a civilian and a military police force and the federal government could only recommend changes, which each state government was then free to implement or ignore.

There was also a deep root of exploitation in Brazil, going back to when the Portuguese first arrived in 1500. Slaves were imported in their hundreds from Africa to run huge estates and to work in the sugar-cane and coffee plantations, and there was much injustice and cruelty towards them. Slavery had been abolished only one hundred years earlier. In 1985 Brazil had come out of twenty-one years of military rule. The military rulers had borrowed heavily from Western banks and by the time Fernando Collor took office in March 1990, Brazil had a domestic deficit of $US25 billion and a foreign debt of $US115 billion. Inflation was more than 80 per cent per month. The country was the eighth economic power in terms of GNP; however, in a population of over 150,000,000 people, seven out of ten Brazilians lived in poverty.

'It all seems so hopeless. Do you think there is a solution?' I asked hesitantly.

'Prayer. Only through God's mercy, Sarah. It is a war, a spiritual war. But as Christians we have the answer, we have the responsibility to pray. Jesus has already won the war against Satan when He died on the cross and rose again three days later. In His name we also have the victory.' She stopped for a few seconds before continuing, 'The thing to do, if you want to help, is not to look at the problem as a whole, otherwise you'll feel powerless to do anything. If everyone in the Church did their small part, a lot of lost and miserable people would be helped,' sighed Myriam.

The two hours flew past and before I knew it I was boarding the flight to Belo Horizonte, having said goodbye to my new Brazilian friend. We would see each other again in three months' time when I returned to Rio.

'Jesus said in John 10 verse 10, 'The thief comes to steal, kill and destroy.' And this is what Satan is doing to the children on the streets today,' explained Johan Lukasse during our first week of lectures.

He went on, 'One third of Brazil's population are under fourteen years old, twenty-five million children are deprived and living in desperate poverty and eight million children are abandoned, needy and walk the streets. Thirty-five per cent of these children die on the streets before they reach the age of eighteen. They are being killed and are killing each other, their childhood is being destroyed and they are destroying themselves with drugs and alcohol, their childhood is being stolen from them and they in turn are stealing. But Jesus said, "I have come that they might have life and life in abundance." And that's exactly why we are here. We are channels for this new life that only Jesus can give them. Why? Because in five years of running this project with these children it is very clear to me that only Jesus can change these children from the inside, only He can heal them from the rejection and the hatred.'

His explanation became horrifyingly clear to me when, for the first time, I went out on the streets of Belo Horizonte to visit the gangs of street kids and saw the terrible reality with my own eyes. Nothing can prepare you for it.

I wrote in my diary that night:

April 5th 1991

O Lord, I was so shocked to see the children and where they live under the freeways in cardboard boxes. The gang we visited were so high on glue and 'tiner' (stronger than paint thinner) that they couldn't walk or speak properly. The whole place stank of urine and faeces. There were about eleven of them in all, only three were girls. The youngest was nine years old and the eldest, the leader, was seventeen. But most of the teenagers looked ten years old through bad nutrition.

Elias, one of the boys, looked just like the Artful Dodger from Oliver Twist. He said he was fourteen but he looked four years younger and spoke like a little old man. He was sniffing emulsion from an old dirty t-shirt and was so high that his eyes were rolling back into his head. Smoking at the same time he tried to make conversation to the six of us and he invited us to sit down on some of the cardboard boxes. Everything was filthy and I noticed that empty bottles of neat alcohol were thrown around their camp amid litter and faeces.

Suddenly the leader appeared from the boxes like a crazy man, roaring and charging like a warrior wanting to kill. The veins in his neck stuck out and every muscle on his filthy and bloodied body was flexed. He had a large knife in his hand and violently jabbed at some of the smaller boys and girls, terrorising them into respecting him. He'd been having sex with one of the girls, Claudia, who emerged behind him so drunk and drugged that she couldn't walk straight. She was about thirteen years old. Most of the girls in these gangs get pregnant when they are twelve or thirteen and have had their second child at fourteen. If the girlfriend of the leader shows interest in

*another boy the leader gets all the other boys of his gang,
even the nine year olds, to rape her as a punishment.*

O Lord, this is the Devil's playground.

*Then suddenly a tall lanky black teenager with a burnt
and withered arm appeared from nowhere with a fresh can
of 'tiner'. They all ran to him and taking a sleeve of their
t-shirts covered it in the strong smelling 'tiner' and sniffed
it desperately. The leader, who had gone back into the
cardboard boxes with Claudia, started to laugh out loud
as if he were the Devil himself and the others started to
join in with him. The noise was deafening.*

*Then all of a sudden I felt the Holy Spirit burning within
me and I couldn't move. I had never sensed so much evil
in my whole life. It was as though I could feel the demons
themselves laughing at us from behind each one of the
children. There was violence, death, destruction. Then the
leader came charging out again from the boxes roaring,
only this time with an empty bottle of neat alcohol in his
hand. He smashed the end off and started charging at his
younger gang members with it. Some couldn't move quick
enough, they were so drugged.*

*The rest of the team wanted to leave. We were afraid.
But I said I thought some should stay and pray, reclaiming
the area and the children for God. Bind and rebuke the
evil spirits with the power and the authority given to us in
the name of Jesus Christ. Karin and I and two others from
our group prayed for a good thirty minutes.*

*There was a noticeable difference in the children after-
wards. Although they were still high, the laughing had
completely stopped and they came to us, quietly asking us
to pray for them.*

O Lord, have mercy on these children, set them free.

You are the Alpha and the Omega. You are victorious. You are the creator of all things. You are so merciful. Set them free, Lord, set them free from the chains of Satan.

God said to me, 'No harm will come to you, Sarah, you are highly protected. Do not let Satan put fear in your heart and mind for the Lord has promised you His protection and He keeps His promises.'

'Be strong and courageous. Do not be afraid or terrified because of them, for the Lord your God goes with you; he will never leave you nor forsake you' (Deut. 31:6).

Where there is God there is love and where there is love there is no fear.

I was living, with the rest of the team from the school, in the Restoration House for boys situated right in the city centre. There were ten teenagers living there at the time, with a few workers who took care of them. The other house, the Rescue House, was the other side of the city and remained open only during the day. Inevitably there was chaos as the children, often between thirty and forty of them, arrived drugged. After lunch they did carpentry before leaving for the streets again. There were social assistants who interviewed the children and teenagers, and a team who visited their families.

By the third month I was frustrated with the language; Portuguese has twenty-one conjugations of every verb. It was very limiting not being able to speak to the children. Also I'd seen enough of kids sleeping out on pavements and in shop doorways, kids knocked down by cars because they were drugged out of their minds, teenagers fighting one another with unrelenting violence, kids stealing from innocent people on the streets. It all seemed too hopeless.

And I began to ask God how He wanted me to reach out to these children. How was it possible to demonstrate to them His incredible love for them, against all the odds?

It wasn't long before my question was answered through a remarkable woman called Debra. She had lived on the streets of New York City for over twenty years and survived. I'd noticed her immediately amongst her team members who were visiting from the States. They had all arrived at the Restoration House one Friday evening to accompany us on our 'night out' with the street kids in the city. She was a big lady in her mid-forties with a mass of thick blondish hair, tied back, and huge brown eyes that seemed to tell a story of someone who had survived the impossible. She had an authority with the children that I'd never seen before, an authority that broke down language barriers as she didn't speak one word of Portuguese.

The extraordinary thing was that as soon as we were all out on the streets she singled me out and said, 'You're going to translate for me.' That was it. I didn't have time to explain that my Portuguese was poor and translating for anyone was out of the question. It was a gentle order.

The children and teenagers flocked around her. I was astounded. None of them knew her past. What was it about her? Then she sat down on a bench in the main square of Belo Horizonte called Praca Sete, and opened the large red bag she was carrying.

'Who needs first aid?' she asked at the top of her booming voice.

I translated as best I could. And the kids responded. Soon she was tending the children, cleaning infected cuts and burns.

I noticed she always used metal pincers. 'Sarah,' she said with directness, 'these kids are always covered in infections. Just by cleaning them thoroughly and applying antiseptic cream and a Band-Aid you will be saving them from worsening circumstances. And never, never use your bare hands. Remember that AIDS exists and on the streets it's rife.'

Then, when she had about fifteen of them around her, she got out her Bible and started to speak to them.

'Kids, I lived on the streets in New York for more than twenty years. You guys are only suffering a half of what I suffered.' There was a gasp from every single one of them. She now had their full, 100 per cent attention. Five more kids joined us.

'I was a prostitute and injected heroin directly into my veins for years. My whole body swelled up and my neck was as thick as a tree trunk. To survive there you have to be tough, and I was. No one messed with me. Eventually the heroin made me go mad and they put me in a loony hospital two years ago. The nurses bandaged up my whole body so that I couldn't move and they kept me in an isolation room with white padding on the walls. I was also dying of cancer.'

Debra spoke slowly to allow me time to translate, which I was somehow managing to do. Portuguese words were coming to my mind that I'd never learnt previously, and I knew I was getting some divine help. There was absolute silence from her audience; all you could hear was the drone of the night traffic in the background. I noticed that the eyes of every child were as big as saucers, completely captivated, and passers-by had stopped to find out what was attracting so many street kids at once.

She continued, 'One day a pastor started to visit me in my isolation room. He was an old man, skinny, with white hair, and he always carried with him a small Bible. He told me that there was someone who loved me unconditionally. In fact this person loved me so much that He had died for me. And that through His death my sins had been forgiven. His name was Jesus.'

Debra paused for a few seconds, looking around at each member of her audience. She was very emotional as she continued, 'I didn't want to listen to the pastor, my sins were too great for anyone to forgive me, let alone Jesus. Also the thought of someone loving me enough to die for me seemed too far-fetched to be true. After all I didn't even love myself. But you know something, this little old pastor kept coming back, every week. Until eventually I began to see Jesus's love for me through the old man. So one day I asked Jesus Christ into my life, I asked for forgiveness for the terrible things I'd done in my past and I asked to be healed, mentally, physically and emotionally. The old pastor placed his hand on my shoulder and prayed for me. Suddenly I felt this warmth passing through my body, I felt the powerful presence of God. And I knew He was real. I knew that I had been forgiven. Two weeks later I was discharged from the hospital by astonished doctors and nurses. I had been completely healed, mentally and physically, of both insanity and cancer.'

Debra opened her Bible and started to read out loud, 'Jesus said, "The thief comes only to steal and kill and destroy; I have come that they may have life and have it to the full" (John 10:10).'

Then, looking up, she continued, 'Kids, the thief is Satan. And I knew him very well for twenty years. He is real too and he only wants to destroy us. But there is only one person who is more powerful than Satan and who can pull us out of his claws of destruction and that is Jesus Christ. I was dying and going to hell; now I am alive and well because of Jesus, who died for each one of you. Listen carefully to what I am telling you tonight. Turn to Jesus, ask Him to rescue you to give you a new life. Ask Him to forgive you, and He will. Ask Him to help you forgive your parents, and He will.'

She stopped and opened her Bible once more and read, 'God has given us eternal life, and this life is in his Son. He who has the Son has life; he who does not have the Son of God does not have life' (1 John 5: 11–12). She prayed for them all and arranged to meet them the following day. Everyone from our team then left to go back to the Restoration House. It was 10.30 p.m.

'We're not going back, Sarah,' said Debra into my ear. 'Life on the streets is just beginning. Come on, let's walk around the city a bit.'

Speechless, I nodded in agreement. And together with another friend, Danielle from my school, we set off for a night I wouldn't forget in a hurry.

By midnight we were seated on a dirty pavement leaning up against a cold damp wall in the poorer part of the city. The area was known as Paper City because it was where the street people brought their cartloads of scraps of paper and cardboard in exchange for a few cruzeiros. The whole place smelt of stale urine.

We were surrounded by other street kids and tramps, most of whom were asleep on pieces of cardboard and newspaper. It was cold and I could see the younger children in the foetal position, trying to tuck their dirty little legs up under their baggy t-shirts in a pathetic attempt to keep warm.

Debra was making conversation with a teenager called Reinaldo who had been on the streets for four years. His long dark hair was matted together and his face, hands and shoeless feet were filthy. The tattered t-shirt and jeans he was wearing stank of body odour. He was drunk and complaining of hunger. Debra opened up her faithful red bag once again and produced a sandwich for her new friend. With a series of *Obrigados* (thank you's), he swallowed the sandwich in three mouthfuls.

Reinaldo offered us each a piece of his newspaper to sit on, which gave a little relief from the damp concrete floor. And Debra continued to tell him her story.

Then all of a sudden three police cars with sirens blaring appeared from nowhere and screeched to a halt only a few feet away from us. My heart skipped a beat and I glanced sideways at Debra to see what she would do.

Six policemen leapt out of their respective cars and ran towards us, pulling out their pistols at the same time. They were shouting, 'Get up on your feet and turn around.'

We did as they ordered. They kicked some of the kids and tramps who were slow to wake up. Then a stocky policeman in glasses came up to us and kicked Reinaldo's legs open and ordered, 'Open your arms as well. Turn your head against the wall.'

The wall felt damp against my cheek. My heart was racing.

Debra started to mouth something at me. Reinaldo was between us and Danielle was the other side of me. There must have been about sixteen of us, all lined up against the wall. I tried desperately to focus on her lips in an attempt to decipher her words. Then I got what she was saying.

'S-t-a-r-t t-o p-r-a-y i-n t-o-n-g-u-e-s.'

I started.

'Who are you?' demanded another policeman directly behind Danielle. He was taller and thinner than the first but his voice was just as aggressive and loud.

'I am a Swiss missionary. We help street children with Youth With A Mission here in Belo Horizonte,' she tried to explain in her poor Portuguese. He started laughing.

Then a terrible realisation came over me. I had forgotten my passport which we were always meant to have on us when on the streets. And I knew that Danielle never carried hers.

'Where are your drugs?' demanded the same policeman, now standing behind Reinaldo. He pulled at the young man and started to frisk him.

'I have none, I have none,' responded Reinaldo defensively.

'These three people are missionaries,' continued Reinaldo. 'Please leave them alone. They only want to help us.'

Meanwhile we continued to pray, under our breath, in tongues. O Lord, I cried out inside my heart, help us please.

The other four policemen were talking aggressively to the other kids who were to our left. The whole atmosphere was terrifying. I had heard awful stories of police brutality to missionaries who were mistaken for drug traffickers.

In the name of Jesus, I cried out inside my heart once more, I rebuke this aggression.

Then all of a sudden the two policemen who were standing behind us completely changed their tone of voice.

The stocky one said, 'Come on, let's go.'

'No,' said the tall, skinny one still standing behind Danielle, 'I want to see her ID.'

My heart sank. She started to search through her pockets. Her hands were shaking.

Then, to my amazement, out of the back of her jeans she produced her small red Swiss passport. That seemed to satisfy them. And they asked nothing from me or Debra. The two policemen returned to their waiting car which still had its orange light flashing and drove off. The other four policemen soon abandoned their victims as well and followed them with a screech of tyres.

We all waited in our uncomfortable positions until they were out of sight.

'Praise God,' said Debra triumphantly, breaking the silence. 'I am so glad that happened.'

Danielle and I looked at her aghast.

'Now you know the power of praying in tongues. Never forget this lesson. You saw with your own eyes that with Jesus by your side you need fear nothing.'

The following morning I woke up early and started to reflect over the previous twenty-four hours. Through Debra I had seen Jesus reaching out to the children. He too had fed the hungry and healed the sick. God's answer to my question was, 'The children are covered in wounds: clean their infections. They are hungry: give them food. They are cold: clothe them. But above all be their friend.'

Later that week, as though in confirmation, I met Marcelo, a beautiful young black man, eighteen years old. He was accompanying our small team out on the streets. We started to make conversation.

'I was a street boy here in Belo Horizonte for nearly six years,' he suddenly said.

I looked into his peaceful eyes and kind, gentle face. It was hard to believe.

'I used to steal, fight and take drugs,' he continued. 'One day, over four years ago, a group of missionaries started visiting the gang I was with. To begin with I didn't want to know them. But eventually I saw that they really loved us because they kept coming back, bringing food and medical help. So I started to become their friend. One day I asked Jesus into my life and I never looked back. I went to a farm far from the city where I recuperated. I loved it there and now I am a worker helping other street boys and girls.'

He stopped and looked at the small group of dirty and drugged street kids we had stopped to talk to.

'Only Jesus can change their lives from the inside. I know because I was there.'

That's it, I thought, that's why I'm here. And once again I renounced all my longings to go back to my comfortable job and home. In July 1991 I took a lift to Rio de Janeiro to live in one of the worst favelas, Borel, with a small team of young missionaries working with Youth With A Mission. There my eyes would be opened as to how these children suffer and to why they eventually run away from their miserable homes to live on the perilous streets of the city below.

5

Borel, Rio de Janeiro:
'They Are Only Children!'

I could hear my name being called over and over again, interspersed with giggles, by the voices of children below my bedroom balcony.

Clearing the drying clothes on the washing line I looked down to find Carla, her younger brother and sister, Vitor and Vivianne, and their friends, Livia and Leticia, looking up at me from the main square of the favela, Borel.

'*Bom Dia*, Sarah,' they all said in unison, their little faces full of smiles. I looked at my watch. It was 8.30 on a Monday morning. The children were on their last few days of school holidays.

'*Bom Dia*,' I replied, feeling more cheerful at seeing them. It was hard to believe that only the day before I had been caught in the middle of crossfire. What kind of future do these new little friends of mine have, I thought to myself, living in a place like this?

'*Vem tomar cafe* [Come and have breakfast]' demanded Carla. She was older than the others at thirteen, and was tall and very skinny due to years of undernourishment. She had a different father to Vivianne and Vitor and looked nothing like them; her skin was blacker and her hair coarser with hundreds of little tight black ringlets. Carla needed affection twenty-four hours a day. She was emotionally disturbed due to her insecure upbringing and spiritually she was in need of a lot of prayer. Her grandmother, who was involved with a *Macumba* (Spiritist) centre, was said to have used Carla as the 'horse' on a number of occasions, which means that the demons spoke through her during the seances. That had now stopped, thank God.

I gave them all a thumbs up sign, and descended the narrow staircase two floors until I reached the kitchen where the old Senhora of the house was eating her breakfast. Anita, the nurse, and I always had our meals with the rest of our small team in the house across the square.

'*Bom Dia,*' said the old Senhora. Her frail bent body, lined black face and grey hair made her look ten years older than her mere fifty years. The Senhora, now a widow, had five children. Aparecida, her youngest daughter, now in her late twenties, and Aparecida's ten-year-old daughter, Priscilla, lived with us, together with Marcelo, a teenager, whom the old lady had adopted when he was a baby. Her two older daughters, both married with children, lived in two smaller houses next door and her eldest son lived with his new wife away from the favela. They were all Christians.

'*Bom Dia, Senhora,*' I replied as I left the house.

The children each greeted me with a hug and fought among themselves to hold my hands as we walked across the busy square. I could feel the early morning sun warming my back. The cloudless blue sky arched itself above us. But as I looked around the square I still felt that same terrifying fear gripping me and I was glad to reach the house on the other side.

The house was surrounded by a high brick wall, more for protection from stray bullets than anything else. As we all tried to squeeze in through the iron gate at the same time I was greeted by more '*Bom Dias*' from Pedro, the team leader, Claudio, Geraldo, Ivan, Anita and Marcia. Breakfast was a half cup of strong, sweet, black coffee and a bread roll with cheesey tasting margarine. But it filled the hole in my stomach and I had already learned to be grateful for every bit of food we had.

Inside, the house consisted of two floors. The first floor had a simple kitchen with a cemented floor and walls. Off the kitchen was a bathroom, the first-aid room and a smaller room where Marcia worked with Carla, Vitor, Vivianne, Livia, Leticia and some of the other children living around us. Another door led to a small veranda at the back with a sink for washing clothes. It was currently home for an ailing dog that Anita had rescued. The dog, apart from everything else, had an upset stomach and the smell when the door wasn't closed made your eyes water. Upstairs there were two bedrooms and a small meeting/prayer room. Everything was very basic and the furniture minimal. Claudio had been in charge of the construction work for the past year.

Marcia had also been part of the team for a year, during which time she had started the small school for the children, teaching Bible stories through art, animation, dance and singing. She had recently left to get married to an Australian missionary, but was back just for the last week of the children's school holidays. In her mid-twenties, she was tall for a Brazilian woman at five foot ten, and was one of the most striking women I'd ever seen. Her long, thick, dark hair fell to her slim waistline and her olive complexion showed off her big almond eyes. She spoke excellent English which was a welcome break for me from my elementary Portuguese.

After breakfast we all came together for a meeting.

'We have no food left in the house,' said Pedro casually. 'So we are going to spend some time thanking God for His daily provision up until now and trust that He will provide our needs for today.'

I was encouraged by his faith. Pedro was full of energy and hardly ever sat down for very long. Twenty-seven years old, of medium height with olive skin and brown curly hair, he had big brown eyes which always reflected the fire he had within. He loved Jesus and he loved the people of Borel. A trained nurse, he made daily visits around the favela to people who were unable to walk to the house.

After about twenty minutes of praying together Pedro asked if one of us wanted to share anything or had a prayer request. My face must have read like a book because Marcia immediately turned to me and asked if I was all right.

'Not really,' I replied honestly. And I went on to explain about the fear that had gripped me ever since the shooting the day before and how I was scared even to walk across the square.

'Sarah,' said Marcia gently, 'exactly the same thing happened to us a year ago when we first opened this house. We arrived during a bad time of shooting and had to come together to pray for strength and courage. It was then that God spoke to us very clearly saying, "I want you to be prepared to die for Me." It wasn't an easy prayer but we knew there was no option if we wanted to stay and be

65

used effectively. And as soon as we'd prayed this prayer the fear left us.'

I couldn't believe what I was hearing. Surely God wasn't asking the same thing from me, I asked myself.

But I knew He was. And then and there I made the most difficult prayer I'd ever had to pray.

'O Lord,' I said out loud, 'I am here because You called me. I'm here because You have a purpose in my life to save some of these suffering children. But I'm scared and that's not right, because Your Word says that Your love casts out all fear. Therefore I declare that I am prepared to die for You. Please use me. I want to do Your will. Fill me once more with Your love for these rejected children. Amen.'

Marcia then prayed for me. Instantly the fear left, and a verse from the Bible came clear into my mind. 'Jesus said, "If anyone would come after me, he must deny himself and take up his cross daily and follow me. For whoever wants to save his life will lose it, but whoever loses his life for me will save it"' (Luke 9: 23, 24). And I knew from that moment that it wasn't me walking around the dangerous favela of Borel, nor was it me going out on to the streets of Rio de Janeiro below to the perilous areas in the city where the street kids hung out; but it was Jesus through me. Therefore I had absolutely nothing to fear.

Suddenly we heard the sound of a horn getting louder and louder and then the screeching of brakes the other side of the wall. We all ran out to find a small van full to the top with fruit and vegetables.

'That was a quick answer to prayer,' said Claudio, grinning from ear to ear. Claudio was always smiling.

It took us all of ten minutes to get everything out and into the kitchen. There were vegetables everywhere.

'Did you hear that Rose went to church last night and asked Jesus to come into her life?' asked Ivan joyfully, as together we carried a sack of potatoes into the house. 'She went because she had witnessed God's protection around her house during the thirty minutes of crossfire yesterday afternoon!' I was thrilled with the good news.

'Sarah,' Anita called me from the first-aid room. 'I want to introduce you to someone.'

Putting down the sack of potatoes I walked into the clinic. A small room, it consisted of a table positioned under the only window, which overlooked the tops of other small box houses, two stools, shelves full of medication (most of which was donated) and a cupboard with bottles of antiseptic lotions and creams, bandages, plasters, gauze, cotton wool, plastic gloves, pincers and scissors. Sitting on one of the stools was a young black man. He had his wounded right foot up on the second stool and was being attended to by Anita.

'Sarah, this is George,' said Anita.

George shyly turned his head towards me and said hello but he couldn't make eye contact.

'George was shot in his ankle last year,' continued Anita. 'The bullet went straight through, as you can see, but it won't heal up. So I have told him to come here every day and we will dress the wound and see if that helps. I was wondering if you could do that for George when you are here?' I was glad that I wasn't squeamish.

'*Sim*,' I replied, only too pleased to be of help. 'It would be a pleasure.'

Anita gave me clear instructions as to what to do and I

said goodbye to my new patient. George and I were to become good friends over the next few months. It turned out that he and his three brothers were members of Borel's *quadrilha* (gangsters) – I felt sorry for their mother – but since he had been wounded he'd been suspended. At the age of eighteen he knew very little apart from drug trafficking and gang warfare.

That same Monday afternoon, members of a local church arrived at the house with bags of rice, beans, sugar, flour, coffee, salt and tea from a supermarket. And three of our neighbours in Borel arrived in the evening with homemade cakes and biscuits. It was all very faith-building because none of them had been told of our needs. In fact, we had so much food by the end of the day that we were able to give some away to families living around us who had little.

Later that week, in the early evening, I went to the city centre to work in a night shelter for young street boys and girls which was situated in a Methodist church near the Rio central train and bus station. The shelter was run by Roberto from Holland and his Brazilian wife. He had rung the main base outside Rio to say that he needed volunteers.

Roberto met me at 6.30 p.m. and took me to meet a gang of young kids that hung out around the central train station. As soon as we reached the top of the escalators from the underground the children saw Roberto. He wasn't easily missed among the Brazilians, being very tall, well-built and blond.

They came running towards us from all directions. Some jumped up on us, others hugged our legs and arms; I literally couldn't move. The night commuters clutched their bags and walked very quickly past us.

The smell of glue made me feel dizzy and my head started to throb. I noticed that one of the boys had a mass of dried thick glue all over his head.

'This is Minerinho,' shouted Roberto to me over the yells of the kids.

I looked round to come face to face with a small, skinny boy about ten years old. His white skin was filthy and his clothes torn and smelly. He looked straight at me with the coldest, angriest eyes I had ever seen. They seemed to reach deep into my soul and I felt myself shiver. Then suddenly I felt the same warmth of the Holy Spirit rising within me, as I had done on a number of occasions before when confronting evil, and I knew instantly that the young boy in front of me was demonically possessed.

As we all set off to the Methodist church, half a kilometre's walk away from the central station, Roberto started to tell me more about Minerinho.

'He is one of the most dangerous and powerful boys on the streets,' Roberto explained. 'He kills. And he is one of the most feared street-gang leaders in the city. He has a hold over the teenagers as well. In fact, many can't survive on the streets without him. He is used a lot by the older drug traffickers in the favelas around here as their *Aviaozinho* [Little Aeroplane]. That means that he is their courier, taking the drugs to their clients and bringing back the money. As a reward they give him cocaine, glue and money. We must pray for him, because once he is off the streets many will follow.'

I watched Minerinho as Roberto spoke about him. And I knew the authority he had over so many kids and teenagers did not come from him, a small, skinny ten year old, but from demonic powers. I also knew, however, from what I'd already seen, that he could be completely transformed by the powerful love of Jesus Christ. Yes, I thought to myself, I will pray for Minerinho. His real name was Luiz Andrea; they called him Minerinho (Little Minas) because he had come to Rio from Belo Horizonte which is in the state of Minas Gerais. Most of the street kids had nicknames for each other.

As we approached a long black tunnel which cut itself through the mountain above us, I looked up at an enormous favela which seemed to stretch itself over the entire mountain from the central train station behind us. It was already dark and lights twinkled from the hundreds and thousands of little box houses.

Following my eyeline, Roberto said seriously, 'Never take any photographs of that favela, in fact of any favela in Rio de Janeiro, because if the quadrilha see you doing this they could mistake you for a reporter. And they won't hesitate to kill.' I was glad I hadn't brought my camera with me.

Once inside the night shelter, which was beside the church, the kids went to take a much-needed shower. There were about sixteen children in all but only three were girls.

'Boys make up 85 per cent of street children,' shouted Roberto as we climbed the stairs to the bathroom. The overbearing noise the children were making echoed around the old house. There was chaos and I began to wonder who really had the control in the shelter, the workers or the kids.

The shelter consisted of a large reception room with a table-football game, a dining room with one large table, and a small kitchen. Upstairs there were two larger bedrooms full of bunk beds for the boys and one smaller bedroom for the girls. The only bathroom was shared by all.

Roberto employed four workers: a cook, a young man to sleep in the boys' room and a woman to sleep in the girls' room. Then there was CaCa, a large black lady, who was a social assistant and worked with the families of the children.

After dinner we all went to bed and Roberto left for home. Minerinho returned to the streets, taking three other boys with him.

I slept on the floor in the girls' bedroom on top of a thin mattress. Telma and Fernanda, two of the street girls, slept either side of me as close as possible on their thin mattresses. The woman worker and another little girl slept on the two bunk beds.

The next morning I woke up before anyone else, bursting to go to the bathroom. But I was pinned to the floor by my two little bedmates who were virtually on top of me. I laughed to myself at the sight we must have made.

After breakfast the kids all had to leave for the streets again. Most did not want to go and my heart broke for them. Adriano, the boy whose head had been covered in dry, thick glue, had had all his hair shaved off by one of the workers. He looked exactly like a young Yul Brynner from *The King and I.*

I said goodbye and set off with nine of the children back to the train station. There were Fernando, Sergio, Adriano, Telma, Isaac, Fernanda, Cristiano, Luis and another Fernando. Most were either brothers and sisters or cousins from the same dangerous favela on the mountain above us, but they preferred to live on the streets rather than at

71

home. They all spent their time around a large rubbish dump situated at the back of the station, along with drug traffickers, prostitutes and tramps. It was a place I would come to know well.

Telma, Fernanda, Isaac and Cristiano held on to my two hands. Sergio held on to my bag and Adriano, Luis and tall Fernando held on to the back of my t-shirt. Meanwhile small Fernando, who threw an easy tantrum, was walking on the other side of the road from us in a huff because there was no room for him. As we came out of the long dark tunnel, many early morning commuters stopped to stare at the crazy foreigner surrounded by so many 'dangerous' street kids.

'Careful,' said one man as he walked past, 'they might steal your bag.'

'No,' I replied, smiling. 'I'm their *tia* [Auntie].' He walked on, shaking his head.

The area around the central train station buzzed like a beehive. On the one side of it there was a large bus station and on the other side there was a popular market. The train station itself was inside a large building full of small liquor and snack bars. It was an excellent place for street people and prostitutes to hang out, both for business and for shelter. Many of the street people set up small tables around the station building and sold biscuits, tins of dried milk, hot dogs, *cachaca* (lethal neat alcohol made from sugar-cane), popcorn and chocolate. Litter was thrown everywhere on the streets; it is hard to find a litter-bin in any Brazilian city!

On the other side of the market-place, across the main street, I noticed a beautiful park. But it was surrounded by a high fence and guards were standing to attention at the

72

smart entrance. It gave me a great idea. 'Kids,' I announced, coming to a sudden standstill, 'let's go to the park.'

They all looked up at me, puzzled.

'We can't go in there,' answered Cristiano with his head down.

'Nothing is impossible with God,' I told them. 'How many of you don't have t-shirts and shoes?' I asked, looking around at each one.

Little Fernando had no shirt, and Adriano, Fernanda and Luis didn't have any shoes.

It was eight in the morning and most of the stallholders in the market-place were only just setting up. But one stall had loads of flip-flops and t-shirts already on display. After another tantrum from Fernando over which colour t-shirt he should have, the amused stall-owner gave me a discount on my small purchases and we all set off for the park.

'O Lord,' I prayed under my breath, 'cover the eyes of the guards and let us pass through the entrance into the park without being stopped. Amen.'

As we crossed the main road and approached the entrance my heart started to beat faster. There were two uniformed armed guards either side of the gate. But I just kept on walking looking straight ahead with the children holding on to me. Until . . .

YES, we'd done it, we had walked straight past them without being stopped.

'Oh, thank you, Lord,' I said out loud. The park was a dramatic contrast to what was on the other side of its high fence. Huge trees with thick trunks and a mass of dark green foliage towered over us and exotic tropical flowers of all colours lined the path we were walking up. Sunbeams shone down through any gap they could find among the thick leaves high above. The children couldn't believe their good fortune. And once we were well out of sight of the guards they started to run and skip and play. We crossed a small quaint bamboo bridge over a pond and the kids stopped to try and spot a goldfish through the murky water below. The sound of the birds muffled the noise of the early morning traffic. It was another world.

I started to teach them a song which they picked up very quickly: '*Deus esta aqui aleluia, Tao certo como o ar que eu respiro, Tao certo como amanha que se levantara, Tao certo como eu te falo e podes me ouvir.*' (God is here, Alleluia, as certain as the air that I breathe, as certain as the sun that will rise tomorrow, as certain as I speak to you and you can hear me.)

I looked back at the nine little street kids dancing and singing behind me and I remembered vividly the original picture God had given me in England a year earlier of the Pied Piper. All at once my heart seemed to burst with joy because I knew I was right where He wanted me to be.

The children ran over to another, larger pond beneath a rock and started to chase some ducks that had waddled away from it. Suddenly before I knew what was happening I saw three armed guards running towards us from different directions.

They were shouting at the top of their voices, 'Get out, get out, you cannot stay here, get out.'

The children ran and hid behind me, terrified that they might be arrested and beaten up.

Then a fourth man appeared, in a suit. He introduced himself as the manager of the park.

'These children cannot stay here,' he said aggressively,

trying to catch his breath. The three other uniformed guards stood behind him, like a back-up team, with their chests out. Hatred was written all over their faces as they looked at the children.

'Who are you?' he demanded, looking at me curiously.

'I am helping to take care of the children. They all stayed last night in a house near by,' I answered nervously, losing all my Portuguese.

'What house?' demanded the manager.

'In the Methodist church,' I replied staunchly.

'Well they can't stay here. Leave by the nearest exit. Now!' He pointed to his left. Then, turning on his heel, he walked in the opposite direction with the three guards following behind him.

The children started to cry and plead with him. 'Oh please can we stay? We won't do anything wrong.'

They were exasperated because for the first time in a long time they were enjoying being children. But he wasn't listening. I started to pray as we turned for the exit.

Then, as clear as ever, I heard God's gentle, calm voice saying inside my thoughts, 'Sarah, they are only children!'

I immediately turned back and shouted at the top of my voice to the manager's back, 'They are only children!'

With that he stopped in his tracks, along with the three guards, turned around and started walking back towards us.

'What did you say?' demanded the manager as he reached us. He was irritated; we were wasting his time.

'They are only children!' I repeated once again, with the authority and confidence of someone who was simply repeating God's own voice.

His irritated expression disappeared. The manager was

lost for words and we all waited patiently until he eventually found some.

'OK, you can stay, but a guard will accompany you.'

The guard he selected looked completely perplexed, but in submission to his boss he led us on a guided tour around the park, dreading, I am sure, the ribbing the other two guards would give him at lunch-break.

The children leapt with joy and thought it was the greatest fun they'd ever had.

Later that morning I caught the underground train back to Saens Pena, the nearest station to Borel, and only four stops from the central station. The kids all wanted to see me off on the train itself and somehow managed to pass more police control in order to reach the platform. Nevertheless, it wasn't long before five uniformed policemen had surged upon us with demands that the kids should leave immediately. However, taken aback by the children's clear distress at saying goodbye to me they allowed time for each one of them to hug and kiss me as the train pulled into the platform. Cristiano, who had been guarding my bag with his life, handed it back to me and I climbed on to the train.

'Who are you?' asked the five astonished policemen through an open window as the train started to pull out.

'I'm a missionary from England,' I replied with a big grin. 'And I'm in Brazil only to help these children.'

Waving goodbye to my nine little waving friends, I couldn't help but notice the policemen's reaction to the little scene. They were, without question, actually touched.

But my joy soon changed to a deep and heavy sadness. As I climbed the exit steps from Saens Pena station to the busy shopping centre above ground I felt tears burning my cheeks. Once I reached the top I sat down on the curb of the pavement alongside the main street and wept and wept, not caring who saw me. I simply couldn't stop.

'O Lord,' I cried, 'what can I do for them? I need a house where they can live and a team of workers to help me.' But the burden of sadness I felt seemed to increase. I was crying now in breathless convulsions from somewhere deep down within me.

Then suddenly various verses came flooding into my thoughts: 'With man this is impossible but with God all things are possible' (Matt. 19:26); 'Cast all your anxiety on him because he cares for you' (1 Pet. 5:7); 'Come to me, all you who are weary and burdened, and I will give you rest. Take my yoke upon you and learn from me, for I am gentle and humble in heart, and you will find rest for your souls. For my yoke is easy and my burden is light' (Matt. 11:28–30). Then I heard that same calm voice in my thoughts, 'Just be, Sarah, just be. Love them, accept them and show Me to them. I, Almighty God, am with you.'

I prayed, 'Lord, I give You back each child. I give You back the sadness. I give You back the burden.' As I prayed the heaviness left me and the joy returned.

While walking the two kilometres back to Borel I realised that God had taught me something that would make all the difference in the work I would do with these children in the future. If I carried all the problems myself and tried to solve them in my own strength I would give up and help no one. If, however, I handed all the problems I encountered back to God and looked to Him to solve them, children's lives and the lives of their families would be changed eternally. In other words, if we did the possible He would do the impossible.

6

Vivianne

It was dark for two o'clock in the afternoon and the rain was still falling although the worst of the storm was over. The air smelt fresher. It was the middle of October, spring in Brazil, but the temperature was around 30°C so we still wore shorts and t-shirts despite the rain. We were drenched, however, and our clothes stuck uncomfortably to our bodies. I noticed through the bus window that the famous landmark of Rio de Janeiro, the Christ Redeemer, was no longer visible, hidden by the thick grey clouds that covered the top of the mountain.

We were on our way to the large rubbish dump situated behind the central train station to visit Telma, Isaac, Fernando and the other street children who hung out there. Gill and Marcos, from my church in Rio, were with me. I preferred not to go out to the streets alone, rather always in twos or threes. First, because it was wiser considering the places and the people I visited and second, the very disciples of Jesus never worked alone so it was pretty obvious what was God's preference.

We always took with us first aid and medication against worms and sarna. Sarna is a terrible skin disease, similar to scabies, that is rife among the street kids. Millions of microscopic germs live just under the surface of the skin, multiplying and spreading with incredible speed. Needless to say I caught it on numerous occasions and can speak with authority on the matter; it itches like mad, especially at night, and can become very painful if not treated quickly. The good news is that there exists a medication called Acarsan, which kills the little blighters within three days if used properly. We could regularly be seen at the back entrance to the station building covering the street kids in Acarsan. They would wash first in water which gushed non-stop from a conveniently burst water-pipe nearby.

The rubbish dump itself was next to a derelict roofless house occupied by the older street boys and girls. Covering an area the size of a tennis court the dump was in what used to be the original garden of the old house. What was left of the original garden wall ran along the back of the dump. Four large alcoves along the length of the wall provided shelter for some of the children. Workmen were always burning large mounds of litter which piled up at regular intervals during the day, so everything and everyone was covered in soot. The smoke from the burning, rotting litter in the hot midday sun was often suffocating. And the inside of my ears and nose were permanently blackened.

Fatima, the mother of Telma and Isaac, also hung out around the dump. She was permanently drunk. Telma was twelve years old and very pretty with fine dark features. Her mother's concern was that her daughter would turn into a prostitute, but it didn't concern her enough to move away from the hellish place she'd brought them all to in the first place. And anyway, for the time being, Roberto's night shelter was preventing her concern from becoming a reality. They had an old filthy sofa which sat on the edge of the rubbish dump against the wall, and two large boxes around one of the alcoves which lent space for a single mattress. Food was cooked over a fire between the sofa and the alcove in a dirty old frying-pan. Fatima spent all the money Telma and Isaac received by begging, on cachaca. She had left the interior of Minas Gerais after her husband had left her for another woman. Her three elder sons had stayed behind and she had picked up her two youngest children and brought them with her to Rio. Isaac, only seven years old, had one of the biggest stomachs of any of the street kids in the area. It was the size of a large pumpkin, full of worms.

Telma would beg all day long carrying a tiny newborn baby belonging to Vanya, a teenage prostitute, who hung out next to the dump with her other daughter of three years old. The baby, Vivianne, was a pathetic sight. At nearly two months old she was dehydrated, covered in sarna and severely undernourished as Vanya didn't want to breast-feed because it would affect her business.

As Gill, Marcos and I approached the dump, having got off the bus in front of the market-place, I suddenly heard my name being called out. Rose, a prostitute who had been selling her body for over fifteen years, came running towards us.

'Sarah, thank God you are here, come quickly, come quickly, follow me please,' she pleaded through frightened, dark eyes. Her matted black hair was drenched as was her strapless mini-dress. Small scars from old wounds covered her bare legs and arms. Her lined black face and toothless grin made her look twenty years older than her mere thirty years.

We followed behind her at a slow run up a dark alleyway

which ran through the middle of old wooden huts where prostitutes and drug traffickers lived, to the right of the derelict house. The rain-water was still pouring down off the roofs of the huts either side of us, and I was glad to be wearing only flip-flops on my feet as we walked through one muddy puddle after another. It was clear something bad had happened, but no one asked any questions. Terrible thoughts started running through my mind: Was it Telma? Had someone died? Was it Vivianne? Or Fernando?

Rose stopped suddenly at the closed wooden door of one of the small huts, about halfway up the alley. I didn't know what to expect and I glanced back at Gill and Marcos, who looked equally concerned. Rose opened the door slowly. It was dark inside and smelt of damp wood, but the opened door threw some light on to the body of a teenage boy lying on the only bed in the room. We walked in and had a closer look at his face to find out who it was. Gill stifled a scream and I closed my eyes quickly, hoping that when I opened them again the bloodied, knifed face before me would have disappeared. It was Anderson, a sixteen-year-old street-drug trafficker. A rival gang member had tried to kill him, Rose explained.

'Please try and do something. He can't go to the hospital because the police will arrest him,' she continued, pleadingly.

'Anderson, can you hear me?' Gill asked in a firm voice.

Anderson stirred, wincing with pain as he woke up. The upper part of his left ear was hanging off and he had deep knife-wounds in his right cheek and forehead. His eyes were stuck together with dried blood.

'He needs a hospital,' said Gill, looking directly at Rose. 'These wounds are deep and he has lost a lot of blood.'

'He can't go, please try and do something.' Rose was getting exasperated.

Gill and I cleaned him up as well as possible with oxygenated water, antiseptic lotion and cream. We placed a lot of plasters across the deep cuts to try and bring the skin together. But he was still losing blood and was starting to lose consciousness.

'Do you believe that Jesus can heal you?' I asked, bending down close to Anderson's good ear.

'*Sim*,' nodded Anderson positively.

The three of us started to pray, not knowing what else we could do to help him.

'*Deus*,' said Marcos, 'we can do no more and therefore we turn to You and ask that You send Your Holy Spirit. In the name of Jesus, heal Anderson's deep wounds, protect them from infection and restore his blood-loss. Amen.' It was a simple prayer and I confess that I prayed it only half-believing that it would be answered. There was a few seconds' silence and all that could be heard was the rain-water dripping down from the roof outside.

Then all of a sudden the tiny wooden hut was filled with an incredible sense of God's presence, so much so that I had to bow my head because I couldn't support the power that was over me. Rose burst into tears. We placed our hands on Anderson and he started to smile from ear to ear.

'Jesus is here,' he managed to say. 'He is healing me!'

We left a weeping Rose with a smiling Anderson and headed back to the bus stop to catch our respective buses home. It was already past four o'clock in the afternoon; the time had flown by.

As I walked back up the steep main road of Borel, which

meandered up the side of the mountain through the very heart of the favela to the main square and beyond, my mind was still on the streets with Anderson. Even though I'd had such little faith God had answered our prayer, I thought to myself. In fact, my mind was so deep in thought that I didn't even notice the smell of the large black ram who lived on the second corner of the main street after the entrance to Borel. He was used in the Macumba centre and looked suitably evil with large black eyes and enormous coiled horns which stuck straight outwards. He smelt like the stink bombs we used to let off at school when I was a kid. I also didn't stop to notice the armed quadrilha who always stood guard on the third corner, nor did I observe the ever-present smell of smoked marijuana. It was only when I was halfway up the steepest part of the next stretch of the road, which led to the fourth corner and the main square, that I happened to look up.

A wave of terror hit me like a bolt of lightning. Coming towards me, almost filling the width of the road, were three of the meanest looking bandidos I'd ever seen, equipped with machineguns, pistols and revolvers. I stopped in my tracks, paralysed, realising there was no one else around. They were practically on top of me now and clearly had no intention of stopping or stepping to the side. Suddenly to my left I heard my name being called loudly.

'Sarah, Sarah, over here, move quickly, over here, Sarah, NOW.'

I looked over to my left and saw my pastor, Willibaldo, hiding behind his old brown VW Beetle, beckoning me over urgently. I moved, in what I recall as slow motion but apparently it was a dash, towards Pastor Willibaldo and his faithful VW.

'Sarah, are you all right?' asked Willibaldo, concerned.

'What's going on?' I asked, terrified.

'They are getting ready for a big fight tonight with Casa Branca. Carlos [I have changed his name for safety] was arrested by the police this morning and the quadrilha here know that they have to get ready for either rival gang warfare or a visit from the civil police. They are sending out for reinforcements as we speak.'

Carlos, at the age of twenty-three, was one of the most powerful and dangerous leaders of Borel's quadrilha and in charge of security and reinforcements. He would visit us occasionally in our house on the main square and Pedro would speak to him over and over again about leaving the favela and starting a new life. But Carlos never listened.

Pastor Willibaldo had lived in Borel for sixteen years. Not because he had to, but because he and his first wife had felt called by God to live and work there. They had helped to start up a Baptist church in Borel off the main square, and his wife had worked with the children. Willibaldo had an incredible love for the bandidos, and I'd already had the pleasure of meeting many who had become Christians through the life of this remarkable pastor and whose lives had been completely transformed. In his mid-forties, Willibaldo was of medium height, stocky with thick brown hair, and his kind brown eyes always reflected his love for Jesus and for the lost. His first wife had died tragically of an illness, leaving him to take care of their only son. Some years later, Willibaldo had met and married Maria, twenty years his junior, and they had two beautiful sons, Gabriel and Rafael, who were both under three years old.

I said goodbye to him and went quickly on my way up

to the clinic on the square, keeping well over to one side of the road by the houses. When I reached the clinic, I found Anita by herself, trying to sweep out the rain-water which had flooded the entire ground floor. I took another broom and we divided the work, with me concentrating on getting the water out from the kitchen through the front door and Anita sweeping the water out of the clinic through the back door.

As we were nearly finishing I went out of the front door to make sure the water was draining away and wouldn't return into the house.

Suddenly, breaking the silence like a clap of thunder, a machinegun opened fire, raining out bullets against the other side of the wall from where I was standing. Like a scared rabbit I dropped the broom and ran into the house screaming.

'Sarah, in here, in here, get down on the floor,' called Anita from the clinic.

I ran into the room, throwing myself on the damp floor. My heart was racing. And I was breathless. It was too much. Surely this was all a movie, it wasn't really happening, I asked myself.

But one thing I knew for sure: the high brick wall around the front of our house had saved my life.

Then all at once we heard the sound of a helicopter coming closer until it was hovering over us. The noise was deafening.

'Stay on the floor,' shouted Anita. 'It's the police and they will shoot at anything that moves down here.'

There was more shooting further up the mountain from where we were. Then after a few minutes we could hear a car driving very fast back down the mountain and past the house through the main square. The helicopter backed off and away until we were left in silence once again.

'Help me, please help me,' cried a man's voice from the other side of our gate.

Anita and I got up off the floor and ran out to see who was there.

'My son has been shot.' There before us stood a terrified young man and in his arms a whimpering little boy of about five years old. 'He was out on the streets just by the square when the police car went past firing bullets all over the place. One ricocheted off the wall and went into his groin.'

Anita led the shaking father into the clinic and he laid his petrified son on the table. She carefully pulled off the child's torn shorts and underwear. And there it was, a bullet intact just under the surface of the skin. It hadn't entered his body and had stopped just short of his genitals. There was little bleeding.

'I think God's hand must have stopped the bullet from entering and killing my son,' said the father, who was as astonished as we were.

'Nothing short of a miracle,' said Anita, agreeing. 'But we need to get him to the hospital to have it removed. In the meantime I will give him some pain killers.'

The father left for the hospital with his son and we walked across the square to our bedrooms on the top floor of the tower-like house. I took a very badly-needed shower before collapsing on my bed.

'Sarah, *ola*, anybody at home?' It was George.

I went into the kitchen and let George in the front door.

'*Ola*, George, *tudo bom*? [how are you?]' I asked, pleased to see my friend.

'I'm fine, but I came to see how you are,' said George, avoiding eye contact.

'I'm surviving, George,' I replied, raising my eyebrows and grinning. 'How can I help you? Do you want me to dress your foot?' I asked teasingly.

'If you have time,' said George shyly, still avoiding eye contact.

'Sure,' I answered, leading him into the small first-aid room. He sat straight down on the stool and started undoing the old bandage from his ankle while I opened the cupboard to find a new bandage, gauze, antiseptic lotion and cream.

'Sarah, I went to church last Sunday,' said George, sounding pleased with himself.

I was thrilled.

'George, that's the best news I've heard all week. How was it?' I asked, putting lotion on a piece of gauze.

'Well, I went to the front of the church and asked for a prayer for my foot,' replied George, actually managing to make eye contact with me. His gentle face broke into a wide smile.

'And?' I asked on.

'It was great,' answered George.

'Are you going back this Sunday?' I asked, looking up from what I was doing.

'Yes, I am,' said George decidedly.

The following weekend, while travelling back on the bus from Copacabana beach, George was murdered. A rival gang member mistook him for his elder brother and stuck a knife into his chest six or seven times. Carla, Vitor and

Vivianne saw everything as they were sitting on the seat behind him. I felt shattered.

That same night the shooting was relentless. Borel's quadrilha were furious and they were retaliating. I held Carla in my arms as she wept uncontrollably for two hours. O Lord, I cried out from inside, what kind of future does she have? No wonder these children run away to the streets below. Please raise up more people to come and help rescue these children from the hell they are living in.

'You're not going to steal from me, are you?' Pastor Willibaldo jokingly asked little Fernando, who was standing by the side of the large rubbish dump on the streets.

'Oh no,' replied Fernando seriously, 'It's terrible to steal from a pastor!'

We all burst into laughter.

I wiped the sweat from my forehead and noticed that it was already covered in soot. The midday sun was well over 30°C and the heat from the burning litter on top of that made the air stifling. It was difficult to breathe.

Gill and Marcos were with me, as were a small Brazilian team from the Youth With A Mission base situated outside the centre of Rio.

'Sarah,' shouted Gill, walking towards me from the derelict house. 'Look at Anderson.'

I was overjoyed to see how quickly he had recovered. It was a week after we'd prayed for him.

'Jesus healed me, Tia,' said Anderson, smiling. 'I'm feeling great.' His deep wounds had completely healed up and it was almost impossible to see any scarring.

Pastor Willibaldo and I were talking to Fatima who was in a terrible state because Roberto had had to close the night shelter. The Methodist church decided they needed the space for their own youth activities! Roberto and his wife had, however, bought a house close by the station which could take up to ten young street boys to live for a time of rehabilitation. Minerinho had been living there for two weeks.

Vanya suddenly arrived holding two-month-old Vivianne casually under one arm. I was shocked when I saw the baby's face. She looked semi-conscious and her big brown eyes were sunken into her tiny face. It wasn't helped by the fact that Vanya had wrapped her in a thick wool blanket which in 30°C heat would make anyone feel unwell.

'She won't let anyone take the baby to hospital,' said Fatima, sighing. 'She doesn't want the baby but won't let anyone else have her either. She only loves Veronica, her other daughter. She is a little crazy, you know. Too many drugs.'

I went over to Vanya and took Vivianne from her. Sitting down on the old dirty sofa I unwrapped the baby from her suffocating blanket. Two of the visiting team members who had sat down with me gasped before I did.

'Oh *Meu Deus*,' I said out loud.

Vanya was laughing, showing us all her toothless grin. Her white mini-dress was torn and covered in soot, her skinny black limbs were covered in marks and small scars.

Vivianne was dying. Wrinkled brown skin hung off her tiny body, her stomach was swollen, chronic sarna, now infected, covered her from head to foot and pus was oozing from her skin. It was particularly bad around the ears, hands and feet. Dried pus made it difficult to open her tiny hands and wispy brown hair stuck to her scalp.

'Let us take her to the hospital,' said Marcos, who had joined us.

'No way,' replied Vanya, still laughing.

'She is suffering and needs help,' said Rubens, one of the visiting team members, firmly.

Anger against Vanya rose up into my heart. O Lord, I cried out from inside, have mercy on this woman for she is out of her mind. Please tell me what to do.

Suddenly into my thoughts came the story of Nehemiah. A mere cup-bearer to the king, when he heard about the destruction of the walls and gates around Jerusalem Nehemiah not only took it upon himself to pray, fast and mourn for the city but, in faith, he went into action to rebuild the city wall. And against all the odds, with a team of officials, merchants, priests and nobles, he managed to do it. All at once I knew that I too had a responsibility, not only to pray, but to act to help save Vivianne's life which was being destroyed.

'Lord,' I said under my breath in English, 'change Vanya's thoughts now. Let her allow me to take care of Vivianne.'

Immediately, looking straight up at Vanya, I said, 'Vivianne is dying, Vanya. She can't stay on the streets. Let me take care of her until she gets better. You can visit her every day in Borel.'

She stopped laughing and looked at me. Everyone was silent.

Eventually she said, looking around at each one of us, 'OK, you can take Vivianne.'

There was a great sigh of relief from everyone, even from the other street children and adults who had joined in the small crowd around the sofa.

Rubens, Marcos and I took the baby to the nearest hospital. After waiting for four hours we eventually left with a prescription for lotion against the sarna, medication to stop her diarrhoea and vomiting and a list of extra nutritious foods to be added to her bottle of milk. The doctor's parting words to us had been, 'She will die if she stays on the street and doesn't receive proper care immediately.'

We eventually arrived back at Borel around 8.30 that night.

Ivan helped me to bath her in a small tub in the kitchen to which we added the lotion against sarna.

'Ivan,' I said, feeling exhausted, 'I have no experience with babies, especially sick babies.'

'Then let's pray and ask for an experienced mother to help you,' said Ivan with a gentle smile.

No sooner had we finished praying than there was a knock on the front door. It was Beth, the Senhora's eldest daughter, who lived next door to me.

'I heard that you'd found a dying baby on the streets and that you've brought her back to take care of her. I was wondering if I could help?'

My eyes were wet as I gave her a big hug.

'Oh yes please, Beth, I don't know where to start.'

Later that night as I lay in bed I looked around my small room, which was lit up by the full moon outside. Next to my cupboard was a baby's bath which Beth had lent me. I was going to have to wake up at two o'clock in the morning to bath Vivianne in the medication once again in order to relieve the itching, and to give her a bottle. Baby clothes, cotton nappies, pins and plastic pants all lay at the ready over my wooden chair. We had given her a bottle full of the ingredients suggested by the doctor but Vivianne had vomited immediately; it was too rich for her sick stomach. Instead, Beth had given her rice milk which she had kept down successfully. Her two o'clock and five o'clock feeds were already prepared in the fridge downstairs.

And at the foot of my bed, fast asleep on a small mattress, lay Vivianne.

'Thank you, Father, for sending Beth. Bless her a thousand times for her kindness,' I said in a whisper. 'But I'm frightened, really frightened, that Vivianne will die. I place her in Your hands and claim her little life for You. Help her, Lord, to recover.'

Then as I closed my eyes to sleep I heard God's gentle, calm voice in my thoughts, 'When she is older she will be a very tall and healthy girl.'

That's extraordinary, I thought to myself, because her mother is tiny. But I smiled because I knew after hearing those words that she would live.

After seven days and seven sleepless nights I was feeling utterly exhausted. Vivianne's clothes and nappies had to be put in boiling water every day to kill the sarna, and I was endlessly at the cooker heating up pots of water. There was no sign of Vanya either. And the thought of Vivianne having to return to the streets was making me feel very low.

I wrote in my diary:

October 31st 1991
O Lord, I'm so miserable. I am so tired, and I'm thinking what am I doing all this for if she is only going to return to that awful place?

Why, God, are you taking me through this experience?

Emotionally I am attached to her. I have nursed her and cared for her for seven days and nights. I have been her mother. And it's so difficult to think that she is going to go back to the rubbish dump on the streets and to her mother who doesn't take care of her.

I am fed up and tired. I'm feeling lonely also. I cannot have a ministry single. I really need a partner, a husband to help.

I believe that I can look after Vivianne for one more week and then she will have to return to her mother. So, Father, change Vanya's heart, or release the little girl to another family for adoption.

O God, please help.

The following morning I left the house in the pouring rain to take Vivianne to the hospital for blood and faeces tests. I'd wrapped her up in some warm clothes and a waterproof mac that a neighbour had given her, and set off down the mountain to catch a bus. As I walked I started to reflect on how generous the people in the favela had been since I'd had Vivianne. She had received more clothes than I knew what to do with. A young mother who lived up the road from us came to the house to breast-feed Vivianne once a day. And the children, Carla, Leticia and Livia, helped me during the afternoons when they got back from school. One little boy had said to me, 'We have a difficult life living here in Borel but Vivianne is even worse off than us, living over a rubbish dump on the streets.'

And that just about summed it up.

As I walked, I heard the voice of Pastor Willibaldo call out my name. He was just getting into his faithful old VW Beetle.

'Sarah, where on earth are you going in this rain?'

'I'm taking the baby to hospital for tests,' I replied, coming to a standstill.

'Well, get in my car and I'll take you both,' said Willibaldo, opening the door for me to get in.

The car engine spluttered to a start and we set off down the steep road to the third corner where the quadrilha guarded the favela.

But instead of driving straight past them, Willibaldo stopped the car and called over one of the bandidos.

'You listen to me, Jose, and listen to me well. GET OUT OF BOREL NOW or you will be dead by tomorrow. Your head is on the block already and you haven't got much time left!' Willibaldo said firmly, waving his index finger at the same time.

'Thanks, Willibaldo,' said a wet and shaking Jose. He threw his cigarette on the floor and stamped it out with his foot as we drove off.

On our way to the hospital my pastor suddenly said, 'Sarah, you are alone in this. The people around you think you're crazy to take care of this little girl, because they don't understand. But God is going to give you a man, a husband who will support you spiritually, emotionally and physically. This man will be able to relate in every way to your past experiences and to your maturity.'

I turned and smiled at Willibaldo. 'Is that a prophecy?' I asked.

'Yes, it is,' he answered, trying to get his windscreen wipers to work faster.

I took a deep breath: 'Willibaldo,' I said, 'I think I may already have met him.'

'Oh yes? Who is he?' asked Willibaldo, taking his eyes off the road and looking at me very intrigued.

'His name is Joao Bosco. I met him at the conference I went to last month in Paraguay. He has worked with Youth With A Mission for seven years, travelling most of the time to other countries around the world. He's an evangelist, full of fire and energy, a man with a banner, someone who should be out front pioneering. He's also taken some courses in video production, in fact he's currently making a video about Youth With A Mission's work with street children in Belo Horizonte. We spent most of the week together talking about our lives.'

'Does he speak English?' asked Willibaldo.

'He does. He's a year older than me and became a Christian when he was twenty-one years old. He was fairly wild before and loved fast cars and motorbikes. In fact he was engaged to be married at the time. Then one night, he had a very bad accident on his motorbike and as he was flying through the air, without a helmet on his head, he saw, as if in a film of his life rushing through his mind, a vision of all his past sins. His whole body went cold and he felt blackness all around him. Suddenly, over a matter of seconds, he heard God's voice saying inside his thoughts, "Give all your life to Me or you will die," so giving his life over to God in his spirit, he then seemed to hear the words, "Put your arms around your head." As he did this he came crashing on to the tarmac road and scraped all the skin and flesh off his arms and elbows. But it had saved his life.' I paused to see if Vivianne was comfortable.

'Go on, go on,' said Willibaldo impatiently.

'This experience changed his life, needless to say. Three

months later he asked Jesus into his life, left his job with the local government, broke off his engagement, sold his properties and gave the money to an orphanage, and bought a small magazine and book stall in Belo Horizonte, where he sold Christian books. He also evangelised with a small team from his stall to over one hundred people a day. After three years he joined Youth With A Mission. The thing that struck me more than anything about him, though, is his incredible faith in God.'

Willibaldo's face broke into a smile. I continued:

'Three months after becoming a Christian he was reading his Bible and praying for his family at his grandmother Felicia's house. His grandmother was ill, suffering from chronic headaches as a result of a brain tumour that had been diagnosed as fatal. He suddenly sensed God telling him to go into the garden, where his grandmother was sitting, and to pray for her. So in faith he obeyed. His grandmother, a devout Catholic, was only too pleased to be prayed for. But Joao told her that if, as he prayed, a film of sins should flash through her mind, she should ask forgiveness from Jesus personally. Then, raising his right hand, he started to exalt God and to rebuke the tumour from her head in the name of Jesus. His aunt, who was watering plants near by, started to laugh and make cynical comments, calling Joao "the little pastor". But Joao kept on praying. Suddenly his grandmother burst into tears and started to confess various sins. All at once, as she spoke out, Joao felt a burning sensation flow down through his right arm to his hand, which he placed over her head. Grandmother Felicia screamed as the heat penetrated through her head, crying out that God was healing her and that the pain had gone. Suddenly, for the first time in her life, she started to speak in tongues and spoke out verses from the Bible. Joao's aunt dropped her watering-can and ran into the house. Two days later Grandmother Felicia was taken to the hospital by Joao's still unbelieving aunt. But the doctors were stunned as every test revealed her completely healed of the cancerous tumour.' As I spoke I felt goose pimples on my arms at the memory of Joao's testimony.

'I look forward to meeting Joao Bosco,' said Willibaldo, parking his VW in front of the hospital.

The waiting-room outside the laboratory was packed and the nurses even suggested we return later in the month. Fortunately I had a form the doctor had given me requesting tests for Vivianne. My worry was that I didn't know for how much longer I would have her and I needed to know if she was better or not. Willibaldo marched straight past everyone and showed the paper to the doctor, explaining the whole situation. Before I knew what was happening the doctors had called Vivianne's name out ahead of everyone else and within five minutes we were leaving the laboratory.

'You will have to come with me to the radio station Boas Novas [Good News], because I have to record my shows by lunch-time, and that doesn't give me time to drive you both back to Borel,' said Willibaldo as the engine sputtered to a start once again.

Boas Novas was a Christian radio station in Rio de Janeiro and Pastor Willibaldo had a five-minute programme, seven days a week. The week's programmes were all recorded on the same morning.

While I was waiting for him outside the door of one of the small recording studios, a woman presenter came up to me and asked who the baby was. Tears started to roll down her face as I shared with her about little Vivianne. 'Wait,' she suddenly said. 'I am currently doing a programme about women working for God, and the message is, "Don't just talk but do something too!" Please can I record a short interview with you now while you are waiting for Pastor Willibaldo?'

'Sure,' I replied, 'but do you think anyone listening will understand what I'm saying?' I asked this in all sincerity. My Portuguese was improving but was certainly not broadcasting quality!

'Of course they will,' she replied, rushing off to get her tape recorder.

A couple of pastors who were also in the radio station at the time overheard the interview and invited me to come and speak in their churches. They wanted to involve their congregations with helping the street children as well. I was overjoyed because it had become clear to me that if the children and their families were to be helped on a long-term basis, the local churches needed to become involved. And while no single church or organisation working in isolation could do much more than scratch the surface of the problem, surely as many as possible working together could become very effective?

The following week Vanya came to Borel and claimed Vivianne. Her tests from the hospital had been all clear. Beth helped me pack up her things and Pastor Willibaldo prayed for them. Vanya said she would take Vivianne to her mother, who lived in Caxias outside the centre of Rio. After she left I went and had a coffee with Willibaldo and Maria.

'Sarah, I know you are sad but you must let go,

otherwise Vanya will start to play with your emotions. Yesterday, I went to visit Fatima by the rubbish dump and I met Vivianne's father,' said Willibaldo, looking straight at me.

'You met her father? What's he like?' I asked, intrigued.

'He's very, very tall and fair-skinned,' Willibaldo explained, accepting a fresh cup of coffee from Maria.

I could feel my face breaking into a big smile. So that's where she's going to get her height from, I thought to myself.

'I was very firm with her father and explained that he had to do something fast if he wanted his daughter to live,' continued the pastor. 'Also I explained that as the father, he had the authority to take her from Vanya and have her adopted. He works, by the way, and probably has another family.' Willibaldo paused to pick up Gabriel, his two-year-old son. 'Anyway, he listened well and said he would do something as soon as possible.'

'Thank you, Willibaldo!' I felt a great weight lifting from my shoulders; and I felt I wanted to tell them my news.

'I've received an invitation from Joao Bosco to go to Belo Horizonte this weekend.'

'You are going, I hope?' asked Maria and Willibaldo in unison.

'I'm thinking about it,' I replied with a smile.

7

Joao Bosco de Carvalho: My Husband and Partner

It was the night of Christmas Eve 1991 and I was having difficulty sleeping. Joao had just asked me to marry him and my mind was full of plans for the future. We were staying for a few days with a Dutch missionary family who had an orphanage two hours' drive outside of Belo Horizonte.

The previous couple of months had gone very quickly. Joao had returned with me to Rio de Janeiro from Belo Horizonte in early November to stand in for his leader, who had been due to teach for a week on a course for urban missions being held at the Youth With A Mission base outside the city. After spending more time together we soon realised that our relationship was more than 'just good friends'.

Joao always says that it was when he came to spend the weekend at Borel and we had to climb the main road through the heart of the favela at eleven o'clock at night that he knew God had a plan for the two of us.

'She was striding ahead of me in the middle of the night and all around us were bandidos with machineguns and revolvers,' Joao is fond of recalling. 'I was scared out of my wits, but Sarah just walked on fearlessly. I'd never seen courage like it before and I remember thinking I could spend the rest of my life with this girl!'

We spent as much time as possible together, commuting between the two cities. One Sunday morning in Belo Horizonte, Joao and I had been praying on his hammock when he suddenly had to leave me alone for an hour or so to sort out some problem in the communications office, where he worked. All at once I heard God's gentle voice in my thoughts, saying, 'Isaiah, chapter 61, verse 3.' Quickly I opened my little red English Bible and read the following: 'They will be called oaks of righteousness, a planting of the Lord for the display of his splendour.' Then I heard God say, 'Share this verse with Joao.'

But I did not do so. When I arrived back in Rio the following morning, I opened my *Living Light* at that day's date, November 26th, 1991, and read once again, to my astonishment, the very same verse: 'They will be called oaks of righteousness, a planting of the Lord for the display of his splendour' Isaiah 61:3. I now knew I must write a letter to Joao and give him the verse. It was my thirty-first birthday!

Two days later I received a phone call from a very excited Joao on a neighbour's telephone in Borel.

'Sarah,' he said in a tone of voice that told me I'd better sit down, 'this verse you gave me in Isaiah, it's incredible.'

'Really?' I did not yet fully understand why.

'Are you reading it in English or Portuguese?' Joao asked.

'English,' I answered, intrigued.

'In Portuguese, "oaks" is *carvalhos*. Carvalho is my last name. So it reads, "They will be called *Carvalhos* of righteousness, a planting of the Lord for the display of his spendour!"'

I could feel my heart starting to beat quickly, and my

face broke into an enormous smile. My neighbour wanted to know the good news.

'That's not all,' continued Joao. 'Over a year ago, when I was engaged and my relationship with my then fiancee started to have problems, feeling very angry and frustrated I asked God one day whether He wanted me to marry at all. He gave me this very verse, Isaiah 61:3, and said that it was related to my marriage and ministry and that my future wife would, in turn, give it to me.'

The hairs on my arms and the back of my neck prickled. I was speechless.

'Sarah?' asked Joao, 'It's incredible, isn't it? God has given us His approval already. I guess He knows us well. Eh?'

'He must have some urgent plans for us both. It's all happening so fast,' I managed to say.

'Don't worry, just trust in God. I love you,' said Joao before hanging up.

A few days later while reading through my diary I found to my astonishment something I had written more than five months earlier, which I'd completely forgotten:

July 7th 1991
This morning I felt God say, 'Stay at the foot of My throne and don't get up and move away. I will bring the partner I have chosen for you to meet you at the same place. You won't have to get up and go to where he is.' A verse really spoke to me today also, Isaiah 61:1–3, but particularly, 'They will be called oaks of righteousness, a planting of the Lord for the display of His splendour.'

In early February 1992 we caught a plane to England and were waved off at Rio's international airport by Pastor

Willibaldo and Wellington and Denise, the leaders of the Youth With A Mission base in Rio. It had been very difficult to say goodbye to my little friends on the streets and I had to give them over and over again to God, trusting that He would take care of each one of them. Also there were now many more local churches involved in helping the children, thanks to the radio station, Boas Novas. And a few of my friends living in Borel, who had joined me on the streets, would be continuing with the work.

My parents were overjoyed to see me again, and to meet their Brazilian future son-in-law. It was a great family reunion. My sister Maria had had another son, Charlie, who was already three months old, and Jack was eighteen months.

Plans went ahead for our wedding on April 4th. It would be my parents' thirty-third anniversary.

'We can either give you a wedding reception, or, if you prefer, we can give you the money instead,' had said my mum and dad generously.

It was tempting to take the money, but after praying we felt God wanted us to have a big celebration so we accepted their offer of lunch at the Hurlingham Club in Fulham, London. We were even given the same reception room where my parents had celebrated their own wedding, thirty-three years earlier!

The night before the big day all my family came together to pray for us. During the time of prayer my uncle, David Aikman, had a powerful prophecy that will remain with us for ever.

'I have chosen you both to rescue the children,' says the Lord. 'Not only the children in Brazil but around the world.'

While he was speaking the prophecy Susan, my aunt and godmother, burst into tears; she had been praying for me for fifteen years before I had become a Christian.

The following morning, April 4th 1992, I opened my bedroom curtains to see a blue sky and sunshine. The weather had been wet and cold the previous weeks and it was a sure sign for me that God was in control.

Holy Trinity Brompton was full of friends and family from around the world. Joao's parents were not with us; his mother had died when he was eleven years old and his ageing father was unable to travel. But his younger brother, Claudio, who lived in New York at the time, was our best man. Nicky Gumbel married us, and friends and family participated in the service, singing songs; praying for our marriage, our future family and our ministry; and of course, reading from Isaiah 61!

Nicky Gumbel spoke to us something I will never forget; he said that a majority of non-Christian marriages were like a box of fireworks that dwindled over the years into a small flame, whereas a Christian marriage was like a small flame that grew in size year after year until it turned into fireworks. He also quoted Isaiah 61:3 and explained that *carvalho* (oak) trees have very deep and strong roots, and that as individuals Joao and I were both strong people and would have to learn to say, 'I'm sorry' quickly to one another.

Forgiveness, he said, would be one of the keys to our successful marriage.

But above all it was the powerful presence of God that made it so special for us both. Many friends who were not Christians were very touched during the service, and my sister Maria and her husband Ed went on to become Christians soon afterwards.

We left the reception on foot, wearing blue and white striped rugby shirts and jeans, with 'JUST' written in red on Joao's back and 'MARRIED' written on mine, much to everyone's amusement. Our first night was spent in a luxurious suite at the Dorchester Hotel overlooking Hyde Park. A good friend of mine who worked for Warner Brothers had managed to get us a less than half-price deal including a bottle of champagne and breakfast, and my granny paid the bill as our wedding gift. The next morning we left for Gstaad in Switzerland, where another friend had lent us her family's beautiful wooden chalet for a week's honeymoon among the snow-capped mountains.

One evening while we were sitting by the fire in the chalet after a delicious cheese fondu, Joao suddenly said that he felt God wanted to speak to us both separately. Leaving me by the warm fire he went into the bedroom to pray. I closed my eyes and asked God to speak to me. Immediately I clearly heard His gentle, calm voice saying, 'I am calling Joao to work with the street children. You will both start a new ministry working with the local churches. The most important part of the ministry will be a farm. I will tell Joao in which city you will start.' After half an hour Joao came back into the sitting room. We grinned at one another.

'It's the children, isn't it?' I asked eagerly.

'Yes, it is. We will start a new ministry specifically reaching out to the street children and their families. It's going to be called *Ministerio Programa Crianca Feliz* or in English, Happy Child Mission. The heart of the programme will be a farm and we will start the work in Belo Horizonte.'

105

'Belo Horizonte?' I asked, surprised. 'Joao, are you sure it's not Rio?'

'No, we will start it in Belo Horizonte. But I also saw a beach with a large stretch of white sand,' continued Joao.

'It's Recife,' I said with a deep conviction.

'Yes, it is. It's Recife. From Belo Horizonte the ministry will one day go on in the future to start in the city of Recife, north Brazil,' confirmed Joao. 'And one day in Mozambique, too,' he prophesied with a big grin.

Before we had met one another God had given us each individually a burden for Mozambique in Africa. A Portuguese-speaking country, it has recently come out of a bloody civil war and millions of children are living in desperate poverty, orphaned because their parents were killed.

We both knelt there and then and prayed with tears pouring down our cheeks, overwhelmed by what God had in store for us and thanking Him for all the children's lives that would be saved in the future.

From Gstaad we went on to Einigen in the German-speaking part of Switzerland, where we did a three-month communications school in a beautiful old castle overlooking Lake Einigen. Joao had been given two free grants to do the course a year earlier, before he'd even met me! It was to be our last three months with Youth With A Mission before leaving to start up Ministerio Programa Crianca Feliz/Happy Child Mission, working alongside the local church.

The main part of the course was producing a research project on how to effectively reach and help 'a small people's group'. We of course chose the street children in

Brazil. The three months gave us time to really research into 'the problem' through studying the history of Brazil (political, social, economic), the children's concept of reality, their social structure amongst themselves and their physical, emotional, spiritual and intellectual needs. From there we spent time praying and discussing a strategy to find 'a solution' to 'the problem'.

It became clearer and clearer to us that the street children needed to be taken out of their city environment and given a new environment where they could become children again. I had seen over the previous year that restoration homes in the city centres produced slow results. Part of the problem was that the 'rescued' street child or teenager often found the transition from being a 'free roamer' to being enclosed in a building difficult to handle. It was easy, too, when the rescue house was in his familiar city territory, to slip away and back to the streets.

We felt that what the child needed initially was to be taken to rural surroundings, a farm ideally, away from the city centre, where he or she could be with animals, work on the land, play sport, and at the same time study at school, learn art and music, carpentry and silk screen printing, and above all hear about God's incredible love and His forgiveness and acceptance.

'But Joao,' I said one night while we were writing the project, 'we can't just go on the streets and choose the children who can or cannot come to the farm. There would be chaos. We need another house in the city where we can get to know the children better and discover more about their families. Many won't even need to go to the farm.'

'Yes, you're right,' agreed Joao. 'We also need to decide what age group we are going to work with. I believe it's between six and fourteen years. Eighty-five per cent of street children are boys, so although we could receive both sexes in the first house in the city, we couldn't have girls and boys on the farm together before we had an excellent structure. They are often sexually active by the age of eight and it could produce more problems than solutions.'

'It's all so daunting,' I said, rubbing my tired eyes.

'But it's not for you to worry, Sarah. Just pray and trust in God because we are not in this alone. In fact there are two large churches in Belo Horizonte that God put on my heart this morning while I was praying; one is the Central Baptist church where I am a member, and the other is the Lagoinha Baptist church which has over five thousand members. So let's keep strong and not look at the normal things man worries about like money, people to work with us, houses, timing and so on, because our only responsibility is to walk on in faith and obedience. God will do the rest, wait and see,' said Joao confidently.

Meanwhile, a local newspaper in England had printed a story about the work I had been doing among the street kids of Rio, and this had led to further articles in magazines and newspapers, and even a radio broadcast in Ireland! Through the generosity of many people, including friends from my local parish church in England, St Mary's in West Horsley, we were able to return to Brazil in September with around $US12,000.

It was, needless to say, very difficult leaving my family. We had no home to go to and no idea of what would lie ahead. There were so many challenges and yet so many uncertainties. We had collected more than five hundred kilos of second-hand clothes and Blue Star Shipping had agreed to ship them, free of charge, to Rio de Janeiro.

Boxing them all up in categories of sexes and ages was exhausting and it was a relief to eventually see them all being driven off from my parents' house to the shipping depot.

The leaders from Holy Trinity Brompton prayed for us both the Sunday before we left England and encouraged us with verses from the Bible, 'You will go out in joy and be led forth in peace; the mountains and hills will burst into song before you, and all the trees of the field will clap their hands. Instead of the thornbush will grow the pine tree, and instead of briers the myrtle will grow. This will be for the Lord's renown, for an everlasting sign, which will not be destroyed' (Isa. 55:12–13).

The next five months, however, were to prove difficult. The Dutch missionary family who owned the orphanage outside Belo Horizonte very kindly offered us a small old house they had on their farm. It had been abandoned for nine years; I will never forget walking into it after a thirty-hour journey from London to find two inches of dust everywhere, a roof that leaked, white walls blackened by insect debris and a shower that only had cold water. To add to our misery, due to a handlers' strike at Rio airport, our suitcases hadn't arrived with us. As it turned out we wouldn't see them again for the next three weeks. The only clothes we had were those on our bodies.

Somehow the grace of God I'd enjoyed every day in Borel had evaporated. Our six months in Europe had spoilt me with the luxuries and comforts I had once renounced. My relationship with God seemed to have changed; it was almost as though He'd disappeared. I couldn't hear His voice and when I read the Bible nothing edified me. It was time once again to renounce my life in order to follow the life God had chosen for me. I remember that a friend had once said that with marriage I would experience a different way of knowing God, as a wife and no longer as His little child. This, I was beginning to realise, would take time to learn.

Joao was back in his own country speaking his mother tongue. I was frustrated because it seemed I'd lost my Portuguese completely, and also the independence which I'd enjoyed for thirty years. There were the expected language differences between us, but also the cultural differences started to surface. The Brazilian culture is event-orientated and not time-orientated. This can be a much more relaxing way to live, but when sixty people turn up for a barbecue at three when you had expected twenty-five people at midday it can be quite a shock initially. Also Brazilians are emotional people who raise their voices constantly when emphasising a point, however small it may be, which sounds as though they are permanently arguing with one another. For instance, if a pastor stands up and shouts his every word at his congregation they seem to enjoy the sermon even more. I always say to overseas missionaries when they first arrive to work with us, 'Learning the culture is more important than the language. Just when you think everything is a disorganised mess it will suddenly all fall into place and work perfectly, only with half the amount of stress.'

After three days of non-stop cleaning, our new little home started to take shape. Joao went full steam ahead with his plans to register Ministerio Programa Crianca Feliz and immediately started to write the organisation's statutes, which I typed on a computer we'd brought with us from the UK. We were both shocked to discover, at a national conference in Sao Paulo for Christian organisations working with street children, that the federal government supported very few, if any, Christian organisations in Brazil. But this did not deter Joao, who made up his mind that once we had set up our mission in Belo Horizonte, he would apply, against whatever odds, for support from the local council.

The country was still in uproar over the resignation of their young 'dynamic' President, Fernando Collor. Accused by his younger brother Pedro in May 1992 of diverting more than five million dollars into personal accounts, Fernando had eventually taken his own leave before being expelled and losing any future chance of being a politician. His campaign treasurer P. C. Farias, who was also accused of participating in this corruption, did not escape so easily. While Collor and his wife ran off to hide in sunny Miami, Farias went on to serve a prison sentence. It was the last thing the Brazilians needed. After twenty-one years of military rule and with a new democratic government, the very man they thought would put them on the straight and narrow had failed them.

In November we travelled to Rio to pick up the boxes of second-hand clothes which had arrived from England. There is a tremendous amount of corruption at the Rio port and often people never see their things again. Initially, the head of immigration told us that all the papers and documents we had were insufficient and that we would have to pay a lot of money if we wanted to see our boxes again. But we were assured again and again by the shipping company that everything was in order. After a tremendous amount of prayer from all our friends in Rio, we eventually witnessed God's intervention.

Returning the next day to the port we met an official who worked in the immigration office, and he also confirmed that our papers were fine. He had obviously enjoyed a boozy lunch and was slurring his words, but he took it upon himself personally to go and talk to the head of immigration on our behalf. Joao and I started to pray in tongues while he was speaking to her. She was saying she would release only half the boxes. We prayed on, and the official continued to plead with her. Suddenly she threw her arms up in the air as though in defeat. With a completely different attitude, she ordered her secretary to type a release-sheet for our five hundred kilos of clothes and called a staff lawyer on the telephone to arrange for her to meet us at the depot to check the boxes immediately. The drunk official gave us a big wink.

As we were about to leave through the main glass doors of the building to walk up to the depot a few hundred yards away, Joao suddenly stopped me and suggested we turn back to the snack bar for something to eat. The timing seemed strange to me because the lawyer was waiting for us, but I agreed. The minute we'd sat down at one of the small tables in the snack bar, which was next to the office of the head of immigration, we suddenly heard a tirade of bullets raining out from a machinegun exactly where we would have been walking. There was screaming and more shooting. We jumped up and ran to the main doors along with a few others. As we reached the glass doors they burst open and two men absolutely white-faced and sweating came running in.

'Bandidos,' said one, trying to catch his breath. 'We were selling fish from our old VW just outside when two of them came up and ordered us to leave the car. Security

112

guards were shooting from behind us, but I managed somehow to hold the end of their machinegun so that the robbers couldn't shoot back and they ran off. Some policemen arrived shooting from another direction, but the bandidos have just stolen another car and escaped. The wall from these main doors as far as the depot is riddled with bullets. Thank God no one was injured,' he concluded as someone led him away to sit down.

More police and port officials had gathered now and someone was crying.

'Sarah,' said Joao, 'It was the Holy Spirit who stopped me at the doors. I didn't know what excuse to give you because I didn't understand, so seeing the sign for the snack bar I suggested we go there.' He took me in his arms; I was shaking and feeling faint.

We distributed more than half the clothes to the local churches and families I knew in Borel and on the rubbish dump. Pastor Willibaldo helped us.

'I have some bad news to tell you,' said Willibaldo. 'Anderson was killed.' I felt devastated. It was always hard to hear that one of the street boys you knew well had been murdered.

In December Joao and I typed up both the statutes for Crianca Feliz and a proposal for the programme itself. There were to be three stages: day-care centre; farm; foster families or their own families. We decided that the farm should never become an institution or an orphanage, but should be a place of restoration, and that to work with the family of each child would be as important as working with the child himself.

One day before Christmas 1992, while I was praying

and fasting, God told me clearly, 'You will have your farm by March of next year.'

It seemed impossible. We had given the $US12,000 raised in England to Youth With A Mission in Rio, as a seed for their future work with street children.

'It's better to sow,' Joao had said to me at the time, as we handed over the money. 'God will give us all we need, wait and see.' His faith was often mind-blowing for me, especially during the first year of our marriage.

I shared with Joao God's words about receiving the farm in March and he immediately announced that although we were penniless we had to start looking in faith at farms for sale around Belo Horizonte.

The more farms we visited the more disillusioned we became. They were either four hours' drive from the city centre, abandoned and in need of a lot of reconstruction, or in the middle of nowhere and too small to take thirty-plus children and fifteen workers.

'God has shown me a picture of a large white house with dark blue shutters,' declared Joao on one of our fruitless visits. 'Nothing is right so far.'

In January we sent out a newsletter to friends and churches in Belo Horizonte with a basic outline of the work we were planning to start and asking for help and advice. A week after sending it out we got a telegram from a man called Helio Valadao, inviting us out for lunch after the service at the Lagoinha church the following Sunday. Helio was an entrepreneur who, together with his wife, ran a very successful bakery and patisserie franchise. He was also the brother of the pastor of Lagoinha Baptist Church, Pastor Marcio Valadao.

There were two thousand people in the Lagoinha church

that Sunday and I remember thinking to myself, Lord it would be wonderful to have this huge church working with us.

'This church has more than fifty-five ministries with the poor,' said Joao in a whisper during Pastor Marcio's talk on forgiveness. 'And this was one of the two churches God spoke to me about while we were in Switzerland. Pastor Marcio is a very humble man of God, and he also has the vision of the kingdom of God.'

Helio and his wife took us to the best Chinese restaurant in the city and he invited Pastor Marcio and his wife, Renata, to join us. During lunch they all wanted to hear about Ministerio Programa Crianca Feliz. While we were enjoying our toffee-bananas and fresh water-melon, Pastor Marcio suddenly started telling us about a farm twenty-eight kilometres from the city centre which his church had bought ten years earlier and which, although still occasionally used for camps and retreats, was semi-abandoned.

'Why don't you and Sarah go and have a look at it? Maybe you can use it a couple of times a year for camps for the street children,' said Pastor Marcio as we left the table.

Joao handed him a copy of our outline plan and we said goodbye.

The following week we drove out to see the farm. After driving for thirty minutes from the city centre we turned off the main road, which continues to Victoria, north of Rio de Janeiro. Passing through an old blue gate we started to descend a stony track which cut through an overgrown banana plantation. The view was breathtaking: great mountains in different shades of green with specks of yellow lay in the distance, while purple flowers massed around us. Palm trees grew strong and tall on the horizon. As we continued down the meandering track a big white house with dark blue windows and shutters came into view. My heart missed a beat!

We were met by Jacob, Pastor Marcio's father-in-law, who lived in a small modern house built especially for him and his wife on the farm four years earlier. He had had a heart operation and needed to leave the busy city to recuperate for a while. They took the reservations from local churches renting the farm for camps at weekends and holidays. Jacob showed us around. Covering an area of around 20.5 hectares (48 acres) the farm was already equipped to take up to one hundred people. The big white house with navy blue shutters had five large bedrooms, two bathrooms, an enormous sitting room and dining room, a kitchen and a veranda. Next to it was an old converted milking barn which served as a refectory. A large industrial kitchen had been built on to the side of the refectory, with a linking hatchway. Below the large kitchen was one of two dormitory blocks with twelve bedrooms and an enormous bathroom with rows of sinks, showers and toilets. Bougainvillaea in shocking pinks, purples and reds grew wild on every visible wall. Looking away from the white house, kitchen, refectory and dormitories, the land stretched downwards over the side of a hill to an overgrown football pitch, fields and a small river which had formed a natural pool deep enough to swim in. An enormous black rock sat dramatically and yet awkwardly next to the pool. Jacob's house was positioned halfway down the hill. The rest of the land on the other side of the big white house was also completely overgrown and there was a considerable amount of work that needed doing all around, but the whole place was ideal for our purpose.

'Joao,' I said, hardly able to control myself, 'This is it, this is our farm. We've got to go and see Pastor Marcio and ask if we can live here and use it full-time.'

Joao was grinning from ear to ear. 'Yes, this is the place. But we are not going to do a thing. If God has spoken to us He will also speak to Pastor Marcio and he will invite us to live here, not the other way around.'

I couldn't believe my ears. But saying goodbye to Jacob and his wife we set off back up through the banana plantation and on to the main road to Belo Horizonte.

It took me over a week to hand back the beautiful farm to God. Totally against all my instincts to act, I had to do nothing; to 'be still'.

Then on top of everything I discovered I was pregnant.

'What are we going to do, Joao?' I asked, concerned. 'We have no money for a doctor or a hospital, no insurance, no permanent home, nothing!'

'So get on your knees and pray,' said Joao, not seeing any problem at all. 'Ask God to provide everything, Sarah. The baby isn't due until October.'

I got on my knees and prayed and prayed and prayed.

The first week of March, Pastor Marcio telephoned and asked to see us in his office that afternoon. And as we sat nervously in front of him he calmly said, 'My dear children. I've read your proposal, and I am convinced that the two of you are not the sort of people who would have given up what you have given up to start this new ministry for street children if it wasn't from God. Therefore, I think you should both go and live on the farm. Sarah, do what

117

you want to the house, make it your own! Fill that place with street children! Initially we will still rent it out to other churches for weekend camps, but let's see what God has planned in the future. Maybe one day you will even buy it from us!'

Joao and I looked at each other with our mouths wide open. We were speechless.

'God bless you both. I am with you all the way,' said Pastor Marcio after he'd prayed for us and for the baby in my womb, asking God to provide everything for our child in His own time.

Two weeks later we moved into the large white house with navy blue windows and shutters. It was March, just as God had promised us, and although there was a ferocious storm our first night and a power cut, we could only praise the Lord for His faithfulness and look forward with anticipation for what He would do next.

8

Ministerio Crianca Feliz/Happy Child Mission: The Valley of Dry Bones

He walked on all fours like a dog, ate under the table like a scared rabbit and laughed into your face like the Devil himself. It was Januario. He was fourteen years old and one of the first boys on the farm. He and his younger brother, Jardel, had been locked in their small, dark, windowless hut for months by their mentally ill mother who thought the police wanted to kill her. Kept alive by neighbours who put food under their front door, the *Prefeitura* (local council) of Sabara had eventually been able to get Jardel out six months earlier. Januario, however, had spent almost a year in total darkness, and he was to the human eye 'insane'. The *Conselho Tutelar* (the branch of the council defending the rights of children and teenagers) did not know what to do with them both and asked us if we could help out. Joao agreed. It was February 1994, and the day-care centre called *Casa Aberta* (Open House), in the basement of the Central Baptist church, had been operating for four months.

When we had visited Pastor Paulo Mazoni of the Central Baptist church seven months earlier he had said to us, 'I believe the farm is the missing link. Our church had a day-care centre operating last year in the basement, but the children would return to the streets at night, as there was

119

no second stage. Also there was no age limit and the eighteen year olds intimidated the ten year olds. Why don't you take over the Centre? It can become part of Crianca Feliz. Use our facilities; there is a large industrial kitchen, bathrooms, a small office, classrooms and a large hall where they can play. In fact, some of the team who worked here last year might well be interested in working for you.'

We were both overwhelmed. The two churches God had put on Joao's heart in Switzerland a year earlier were indeed working with us, and 100 per cent. Selma, Josey, Marcos and Pedro, who'd worked in the Centre the previous year, joined us. A mature lady in her late thirties, Selma's mother-heart and administrative skills made her the obvious candidate for the job of co-ordinator. Although Joao and I would remain the overall leaders, we needed someone both on the farm and in the Centre who could supervise the daily programmes.

We all met up regularly to pray and fast together and slowly the team started to increase. Iona from Recife, who had been with Operation Mobilization, joined us on the farm, as did Ricardo, a good friend of Joao's from Youth With A Mission, who became the farm co-ordinator, and Mauro from the Lagoinha church. Leia, Claudia, Carla and Rubens joined also to work in the day-care centre. There was no question that if the ministry was to grow and multiply then deep roots had to be planted; there had to be a solid foundation. The work God wanted to do in these children's lives would only be eternal if the foundation was strong. This would be achieved through one thing only: prayer.

By the end of August, however, we still did not have the finance to open the Centre. It had been supported the previous year by the Prefeitura and we had reapplied, but the bureaucracy and paperwork was slow and complicated. Compassion International, an American Christian organisation financing work with children in third world countries, had come to visit Joao and me on the farm in August. Derci, the Brazilian director, had been very encouraging although there was no promise of financial help.

At the beginning of September Joao received a phone call from Luis, a church deacon on the committee at the Central Baptist church. His heart sank as Luis told him, 'As you are still not using the church's facilities for the street children we would like to use them for our crèche. The house we have for the crèche in the favela needs painting and some construction work, so they are going to move into the church itself. Sorry for the inconvenience.'

Distraught, Joao and I called for an urgent prayer meeting at the farm. At the end of it Joao suddenly announced, 'We will go and see Luis, Pastor Paulo and the rest of the committee at the church this evening and tell them that we will be opening the day-care centre there next week. Let's all take a step of faith; maybe that's what God is waiting for. He will have to provide.' We all looked at him aghast, but no one resisted because deep in our hearts we knew there was no option. We all had to take a step of faith.

That night, after returning triumphantly from the meeting with the church committee where Pastor Paulo had given us all his unequivocal support, I opened my Bible and started to read from the book of Joshua in the Old Testament, where Joshua was faced with the challenge of getting hundreds and thousands of Israelites, their belongings, all the animals and the ark of the Lord across the fast-flowing Jordan river on their final stage of reaching the Promised Land. Suddenly the following words jumped out at me from the pages: 'And the Lord said to Joshua, "Today I will begin to exalt you in the eyes of all Israel, so that they may know that I am with you as I was with Moses. Tell the priests who carry the ark of the covenant: 'When you reach the edge of the Jordan's waters, go and stand in the river.'"' (Joshua 3:7–8).

As I read on my heart was filled with a sudden joy.

Now the Jordan is in flood all during harvest. Yet as soon as the priests who carried the ark reached the Jordan and their feet touched the water's edge, the water from upstream stopped flowing ... The priests who carried the ark of the covenant of the Lord stood firm on dry ground in the middle of the Jordan, while all Israel passed by until the whole nation had completed the crossing on dry ground (Joshua 3:15,16a,17).

All at once I just knew that we had to have taken this step of faith in order for God to release the finance we needed. Now we had to wait for God to act. There were five days left before we would be opening Casa Aberta.

The following day while Joao and I were having lunch at the farm we suddenly heard the sound of a car engine approaching the farm house through the banana planta-tion. Leaving the table, Joao went to see who it was.

'It's Derci, from Compassion International,' exclaimed Joao from the front door.

'This is unexpected,' he continued as he took Derci's

hand and invited him in to have lunch with us. Derci, a small man with a permanent smile, kissed me on each cheek and seated himself at the head of the table between Joao and me.'

'So,' said Derci as he placed a ladleful of *feigao* (beans) on to his plate, 'when are you starting?'

Joao and I looked at each other across the table, wide-eyed. We quickly filled him in with the situation at the Central Baptist church and explained that we had five days to start the day-care centre.

'Good, good,' continued Derci, still smiling, as he started to attack his plateful of rice, beans, mashed potato, chicken and salad. 'So let's work out what you've got and what you need.'

After the plates were cleared away Derci took a pen and a sheet of paper and wrote out the names of the ten people ready to work in the Centre, including a cook and a cleaner. We estimated that initially around twenty street children would attend the Centre daily Mondays to Fridays which, including the workers, would mean feeding just over one hundred mouths both breakfast and lunch per week. Plus we needed to buy paper, paints, crayons and games for the children to play with, and toiletries for the bathroom, towels and cleaning products. The kitchen was equipped with the basics, but the small office needed stationery, a filing cabinet, a typewriter and a telephone. We also wanted to give the team a monthly offering, not a salary. If Joao and I would be living by faith then it was important that the team were too. Fully aware of the difficulties the majority of Brazilian missionaries have in finding personal financial support from the local church, we wanted to be able to help. But for each one of our team members it meant renouncing the security of a good monthly salary and trusting fully in God to supply their needs.

'Well,' concluded Derci, 'I calculate that you require around $US2,250 per month initially to start the Centre. This also includes an offering of $100 to each worker plus bus tickets. My question is, though, where will these children sleep at night? Yes, I understand that soon many will be coming here to the farm for a time of restoration, but while you are trying to find their families or preparing them to come to the farm they'll need a place to sleep.'

'Yes,' said Joao in agreement. 'We will have to get praying for a night shelter in the city centre.'

'*Tudo tem a hora certa* [everything in its right time]. God knows what's needed better than we do,' concluded Derci. 'Anyway, on to solving today's problem: Compassion International are with you all the way and we will have $US2,250 in your account by Monday, and every month for eleven months thereafter. The contract will be reviewed and hopefully renewed yearly. We will require a monthly report of how the money is spent and also what has happened, in detail, with the work in the Centre. Remember, we will be praying for you all.' He gave us both a big, brotherly hug and, with tears in his eyes, Joao prayed and thanked God for His incredible faithfulness.

We had taken a step of faith and He had honoured us within twenty-four hours.

Casa Aberta opened on September 18th 1993, taking in both girls and boys between the ages of six and fourteen years. The first four months provided us with some challenges. We were all learning and discovering the best programme for the children during the day; the importance of unity in the team; the importance of prayer daily both before the children arrived in the morning and when they'd left in the afternoon. The Centre is our first point of contact with the street children. They are coming in directly from the streets and bringing with them violence, anger, hate, prostitution. It is a place of high agitation. It is a place of spiritual warfare as there they come to hear of Jesus Christ and His love for them for the first time.

Windows and furniture were broken weekly. A policeman had to be on guard outside the church full-time to prevent fights or complaints from the neighbourhood. Two boys were caught having sex with each other in the bathroom.

The team had problems among themselves, gossip started, complaints, doubts about whether God would really take care of them financially, criticisms about leadership. Satan was at work to divide unity, to try and prevent God's will from taking place both in the children's lives and through the lives of the workers. But it was a time of growth as we came together to pray and fast, to confess and ask for forgiveness from one another. A meeting was started every Friday for the team in the Centre called '*Lavando roupas sujos*' ('washing dirty clothes'!); it was a time spent together openly confessing bad attitudes, irritations, hurts and misunderstandings between one another. It was a humbling experience and was to prove essential if unity was to prevail; 'How good and pleasant it is when brothers live together in unity! It is like precious oil poured on the head, running down on Aaron's beard, down upon the collar of his robes. It is as if the dew of Hermon were falling on Mount Zion. For there the Lord bestows his blessing, even life for evermore' (Psalm 133).

At that time the centre was opening at 07.00 and closing at 19.00. There was a shift of four workers in the morning and four in the afternoon. The kids took a shower as soon as they arrived, then followed it with breakfast. In the mornings before lunch they would play games and in the afternoons they would do artwork and hear about the love of Jesus through storyboards, puppet shows and dramas teaching forgiveness and salvation. A team also went out on the streets in the early morning Monday to Friday and on Monday nights. It was essential to understand 'their world', 'their home'; if not the Casa Aberta didn't function. In the Casa Aberta the children were made aware that they needed to change, that they had to follow our schedule and comply with 'our limits' and 'our rules'. On the streets 'their rules' were the opposite of ours: they had to steal for their gang leader, they had to take drugs, they had to swear and speak 'the street language', they had to fight to survive.

Mark Hester, one of the first of many overseas short-term missionaries, came out to help us at the time of the opening of the Centre. He was to prove a very faithful friend and to play a strategic part in the growth of Happy Child in the future. He'd started writing to Joao and me and praying for the children a year earlier. One letter really touched me. He'd been on his way out shopping to buy a pair of trainers, when God put it on his heart to send the money to us instead, to buy a pair of trainers for one of the kids who had no shoes at all.

Our first son, Lucas, had been born on October 26th and once again we'd seen God's provision. Three weeks before he was born we had moved into the small modern house on the farm vacated by Jacob and his wife who had moved back to live in the city. This was a blessing because the main white house was filling up with workers, and as leaders we needed our own nest. The week before Lucas was born we still did not have money to pay the doctor and the hospital bills. Then, unannounced, a deacon from the Community Church, where Joao and I are members, arrived at the farm. He handed us a cheque, explaining that during a prayer meeting at the church the previous night God had told them to give us an offering especially for our baby. We had not told them of our need. The cheque was for a considerable amount of money and I remember feeling completely overwhelmed by the whole situation. God seems to wait until the last hour, but He never fails us. That night I read, 'And without faith it is impossible to please God' (Hebrews 11:6a).

That same February in 1994, along with Januario and Jardel, nine other boys arrived at the farm: Oades, Welbert, Kleber, Adriano, Eduardo, Cristiano and Jose Roberto from the Casa Aberta, Marcos Silva through the Conselho Tutelar and Joao Carlos from the restoration house at Youth With A Mission. Also a little girl, ten-year-old Giselle, was living with Joao and me in our house. She had been taken to the Casa Aberta by the Conselho Tutelar on her way to the FEBEM, an overcrowded house for girls and boys run by the Government. Her father was a tramp on the streets of Belo and had threatened to kill her; her mother had been murdered on the streets of Sao Paulo by a lover. When Joao and I saw her sitting all alone reading a book with her small plastic bag of belongings beside her, we looked at each other in silent agreement. She stayed with us for three months before being fostered by a family in the first 'family foster home'.

Oades, born in Bahia in north Brazil, was thirteen years old at the time he arrived on the farm. His mother, a teenager when she gave birth to him, lived in an orphanage, but she soon left him with the elderly couple running the home. Eventually they sent him to Belo Horizonte when he was eleven years old to live in *Cidade do Menor*, a government house for children and teenagers; apparently he was 'causing problems'. Oades hated his new home and spent the next two years living on and off the streets. He slept in shop doorways and under freeways. He stole to buy marijuana, glue and solvent. He was sexually abused and abused others, of both the same and the opposite sex. At the time he arrived on the farm he hadn't heard from his mother for six years; for all he knew she was dead. He never knew his father.

Small and skinny for his thirteen years, Oades was an artist. Drawing from memory, his brilliant and creative sketches and paintings always attracted the attention he so desperately sought from others. His large almond eyes and mouth smiled with pride as once more he showed off his latest picture. But Oades had the capacity to charm you and then sting you. Beneath the sweet smile he was angry. Rejected by his mother, he felt alone.

'I have no one,' he said to me once through tears, at the end of a week of bad moods and angry tantrums. 'Not even my tia cares about me any more.'

His own inferiority complex made him a cynic, and he could cut people down to size with perfect timing and precision.

'The first thing we are going to do with Oades,' said

Joao during one of our first team meetings, 'is to value him for who he is and not for what he can do.'

Welbert was fourteen years old when he arrived. He had spent three years living on the streets. We'd made a deal with him that before coming to the farm he had to spend one week sleeping with his mother and four brothers and sisters in their tiny two-roomed house, returning to the Casa Aberta during the day. This was important for Welbert because his mother had visited the Centre on a number of occasions for help, and although it wasn't feasible for him to live permanently with her because of severe poverty, bad relations, emotional hurts and his own need for restoration, Welbert had to give value to his family before making his commitment with us. Medium height and stocky with brown skin, tight curly hair and small eyes, Welbert was one of the most aggressive boys on the streets. He was arrogant, over-competitive, temperamental and very strong-willed. His small two-roomed home in Palmital, one of the poorest favelas in Belo Horizonte, was a place of arguments and fighting. At the age of five he caught his father in bed with another woman and from that moment on he decided to face life alone. He didn't need his parents, he would take control of his own life. His aggression and bullying worsened as he grew older. He told me later, 'Whenever I went home there was no love, no affection, no peace, and so I decided to stay on the streets where at least I had friends. But I had no happiness, only a deep hate for life.'

Joining one of the most dangerous gangs in the city he became street smart, he could outrun the police. By the age of twelve, stealing, sex, drugs and death threats were his lifestyle. He went to prison, was tortured by another gang leader who burnt his arms and chest with a lit cigarette and was persecuted for months by a death threat from another gang leader which meant he couldn't ever sleep peacefully at night: one form of murder was to set fire to your rival as he slept.

Eduardo and Cristiano were brothers. Eduardo was thirteen and Cristiano eleven when they arrived. They had been born in Belo Horizonte in a very poor part of town; their two-roomed house was home for a family of ten children. At the age of two Eduardo was taken to the FEBEM children's home by his parents. But his aunt went and got him out and took him to live with her. Eduardo never forgot the rejection he felt from his parents and this had turned into a deep anger and anxiety. From the age of eight he divided his time between living on the streets and with his family. Stealing from pedestrians became his hobby and the goods were sold to store sellers in the main bus station in order to buy drugs. But Eduardo wanted to change.

Cristiano had followed him to the streets a year earlier. He had been hit by a car which had left him with a nasty scar on his right foot. He was often sulky and enjoyed provoking a fight.

They looked alike, stocky and muscular with black velvet skin and a big white smile.

Jose Roberto, known as Ze, was big for his twelve years. He was nervous and stuttered when he arrived. His gentle face was a mask for a deep hate for life and everything around him. All he spoke about was death, accidents and

130

morbid stories. He didn't like his mother; she had taken him to the Cidade do Menor when he was only six years old. She currently lived in a tiny two-bedroomed house in Taquaril, the most dangerous favela in the city, with no water and no electricity. Her lavatory was a hole in the ground and Ze was embarrassed by her poverty. On a visit to his mother's tiny but spotlessly clean house ten months later, Joao said to Ze, 'After God, your mother is the most precious thing in this world. She gave birth to you, Ze. Forgive her and accept her.' She was very proud of him and introduced him to all her neighbours as a pastor!

His tall musical father had died of alcoholic poisoning when he was a baby. In the Cidade do Menor Ze was abused physically and sexually, once so badly that he ran away to the woods where he stayed alone for two nights. 'I cried a lot, and felt very angry,' he recalled. It was painful to remember. For six years he divided his time between living on the streets and in the Government house. Although well behind for his age at school because of his past life, Ze was intelligent and had inherited his father's musical talents.

Marcos Silva's skinny, tiny frame, brown skin, mass of thick black hair and big brown eyes reminded me of Mowgli from Walt Disney's cartoon film *The Jungle Book*. He had come to us through the Conselho Tutelar because his drunk and violent father had knifed him in the scalp. The judge had prohibited the father access to Marcos until ruled otherwise. Marcos had run away to the streets along with his sister who was taken to the FEBEM by the Tutelar. His mother had apparently escaped to the interior of the state with his other brothers and sisters.

Marcos cried constantly and wet his bed every night. He was ten years old.

Joao Carlos had run away from Youth With A Mission's restoration house twice and he was referred to us. He was fourteen years old and his appearance was not one of a street boy. Tall and attractive with a charming smile, Joao Carlos was always immaculately dressed. But he could manipulate anyone, lying with a cool arrogance which at times made it difficult to know who you were really dealing with. His mother had left him and his sister when they were young and his father had married again. However, Joao Carlos and his stepmother fought constantly and eventually he had run away to the streets where he'd made an old abandoned car his home. Youth With A Mission had taken him in to live in their restoration house. As a result of this he was accustomed to having his day scheduled and he had an understanding of the love of Jesus. But his strong will often made it difficult to help him because he wasn't prepared to submit easily. After one day on the farm, however, he came and asked Joao and me if he could stay on. He needed the wide open spaces.

Kleber had come from the interior of Minas Gerais where his alcoholic mother had brought up both him and his elder brother single-handed. His brother grew up to become a professional robber and Kleber his accomplice. They had been caught once and sent to prison. When Kleber was let out they sent him on to the Cidade do Menor in Belo Horizonte. There his best friend was Adriano, the most violent and abusive boy in the home. Although they were both aged fourteen they were opposites in character. Kleber's shy awkward manner hid the anger and aggression bottled up inside which Adriano could express for him with ease. They were inseparable, and arrived together at the Casa Aberta. The Prefeitura had set up a department called PROMAN specifically to provide work and training opportunities for street boys and girls with the state companies in the city. Two opportunities opened up with CEMEG (the electricity board) and we put forward Kleber and Adriano, who were both accepted.

Adriano had been thrown out of every home and organisation for boys in the city. He was labelled 'impossible'. He was born in a small town twenty kilometres' drive from Belo Horizonte, and his mother had died when he was a baby, leaving him with his alcoholic and violent father. His father's furious temper had been taken out on Adriano for most of his childhood and the beatings he'd taken had been so severe that one almost suspected slight brain damage as a result. Tall and lanky with large sticking-out ears and small scars on his white face, Adriano had to have 100 per cent attention at all times; he had to be in control. To this end he had adopted the same violent attitude as his father, to terrify those around him into submission. Adriano was to cause us a tremendous amount of trouble in his first four weeks, because he didn't want to change, he didn't want help. He beat the other boys; he fought physically with Ricardo and Mauro who are both tall for Brazilian men at six foot three and four inches respectively. Eventually he challenged Joao's and my leadership, intimidating all the boys to speak 'his language' and obey 'his orders', not ours. The final straw came one night when he physically attacked Joao, pulling him to the ground in front of the others. We had to make a quick decision, because we were helping no one. The next day we managed to locate his father who was remarried, reformed from alcohol and now employed as an ambulance driver. He'd been looking for Adriano and wanted to start over again as his father. Silvia, a Christian psychologist working in the Casa Aberta with the families, agreed to follow the case with bi-weekly therapy. As soon as Adriano left the farm the whole atmosphere changed.

'Two of the things that can give back a person's dignity are work and responsibility,' said Joao as we planned the programme for the farm. 'The boys must all have daily duties here on the farm and they must help us in all we do here on the land: building the warehouse, starting a vegetable garden, taking care of the horses, chickens, banana plantation and so on. And they must all go to school.'

We had received an offering of \$US5,000 from the Besom Foundation in England towards a much-needed new building on the farm. The 300 square metre Warehouse (as we call it) with seven rooms plus lavatories would be used for classrooms where the children could receive extra tuition and where they'd learn art, music and carpentry. Although the offering wasn't enough to complete the building project we decided in faith to start, trusting that God would provide the extra \$15,000, which of course in due time He did.

Pastor Marcelino, who was also a builder, had joined us on the farm to construct it, along with Ailton. Marcelino lived on the farm during the week and returned to his wife and three sons at weekends. They lived in Sabara, a city outside Belo Horizonte about one and a half hours' drive from the farm. He also took the role of pastor during the services we held on Wednesday nights. Ailton and his wife and two small sons also came from Sabara but Ailton's life was under threat from a drug trafficker who had murdered his brother a month earlier. They needed to move away for a while and Joao and I offered them a small outhouse on the farm. He was an excellent builder and his wife, Marina, became the second cook in the kitchen.

The main cook was Maria. A woman in her late forties with seven children, she walked every day from Ravena, the local village, about one and a half kilometres from the farm. She soon became a Christian, having led a miserable life with a difficult twenty-five year marriage. But her husband was to follow her decision and God started to restore their marriage. Two years later in September 1995 their small home was to become the location for a discipleship group. Tonica, also from Ravena, joined us to clean the main house and the children's clothes, and Vilma came to help Joao and me in our house and with Lucas.

The local school in Ravena with around four hundred students only went up to the end of the *Primeiro Grau* (First Grade). The Primeiro Grau consisted of eight years of study and pre-school, supposedly starting at the age of five and finishing at the age of fourteen. Those wanting to study the *Segundo Grau* (Second Grade), which was three years of study from the age of fifteen to eighteen, had to go to Belo Horizonte. Very few went to university. A majority of the street children have never been to school and most of the boys on the farm were only in the first or second year of the Primeiro Grau even though they were thirteen or fourteen years old. Gilberto Dimenstein writes in his book *Brazil: War on Children,*

Four million of Brazil's thirty-one million school-age children have never been to school. Of the twenty-five million who go, usually studying in overcrowded, dilapidated buildings for no more than three or four hours a day, fifteen million drop out before the end of the fourth year. Only five million finish the full eight years of first grade and, of these, just three million complete their secondary school education. In 1967, 7.4 per cent of the children who began school went on to higher education. In 1989 the proportion had fallen to only 5.9 per cent.

Penha, the director of the school, was in need of help. The state had guaranteed her new chairs and desks on the condition that the construction of a new classroom was completed by the beginning of March. When Joao went to speak to her about the possibility of accepting eleven ex-street boys to study that year she had only one week left to finish the job. Joao spoke to Pastor Marcelino and Ailton, who offered their services wholeheartedly and managed to finish the classroom with one day to spare! The eleven places were given unconditionally and any others needed thereafter.

All the boys apart from Oades and Joao Carlos were studying the first and second years in the afternoons from 12.30 until 16.30. Oades, studying the third year, and Joao Carlos, the sixth, went to school in the mornings from 07.00 until 11.00. Their first day at school was a day of celebration as they set off by foot with new school bags, new white t-shirts, jeans and trainers!

The weekly schedule played an important part in their restoration. It was time to put limits in their lives, our limits. There had to be a time to play, to study, to work, to rest, to pray and read the Bible, to go on outings. They had to learn about hygiene; making their beds, washing their underwear, cleaning their bedrooms, taking a shower daily, brushing their teeth with toothpaste. Their bedrooms in the outside dormitory, next to the main kitchen and refectory, slept four to a room and each boy had his own cupboard with a lock. Ricardo and Mauro took it in turns sleeping with them at night. They had to learn to eat three times a day at specific times: breakfast at 07.30, lunch at 12.00, dinner at 19.00. They had to understand that asking for third and fourth helpings was not necessary because they could be sure of getting a snack at tea-time and a full meal at dinner-time. On the streets they never knew when they'd get their next meal. Most had never eaten at a table and they had to be taught how to eat with a knife and fork. They had to learn manners: when to say please and thank you; to wait their turn; how to ask for something they wanted without grabbing it or demanding it; how to ask for forgiveness from one another instead of fighting or holding a grudge. We had to teach them to ask one of us, the workers, to resolve their problems or arguments before they turned into a fight.

'Sarah, Sarah,' cried Cristiano, 'Marcos went into my cupboard and stole my t-shirt.'

'It's my t-shirt and your cupboard was open. Anyway he called me a son-of-a-bitch,' screamed back Marcos.

'OK, OK, calm down,' I said, sitting down and gesturing for them to sit down next to me. 'Who do you both think is wrong here?' I asked.

There were a few seconds of silence.

'He stole my t-shirt,' continued Cristiano, not making eye contact.

'Cristiano called me a son-of-a-bitch,' shouted Marcos, looking in the opposite direction.

'So who's got to ask for forgiveness here?' I asked on.

There were a few more seconds of silence.

'I'm sorry I took your t-shirt, but I thought it was mine and anyway your cupboard was open,' said Marcos, looking down at his feet.

'Look at each other, guys,' I suggested.

'I forgive you,' replied Cristiano, trying to make eye contact. 'And I'm sorry I called you a son-of-a-bitch.'

'*Esta Perdoado* [You are forgiven],' answered Marcos with a grin.

As with any family there had to be rules and disciplines; after all we were legally their guardians. They couldn't swear, smoke, take drugs, fight or answer back at the workers. They had to co-operate with the daily schedule. On the moral side they had to understand that sex between them was not right and that God created man to be with woman and at the right time, when they were older and married. But discipline with love makes a big difference.

Late one Friday night during the first few months at the farm, Joao was returning from Belo Horizonte when he found all the boys outside their dormitory screaming, shouting and cheering at Ze and Cristiano who were fighting with fury. Poor Pastor Marcelino was trying to gain control, without success. As soon as they saw Joao they all fell quiet, except for Ze and Cristiano who were spitting and swearing at each other with terrific anger. Joao intervened and sent them all to bed, telling the two fighters that any more sound out of them and they'd be disciplined. Then without their knowing Joao stayed outside their bedroom door and he overheard Ze threatening to kill Cristiano. He burst into the room taking them by surprise and disciplined Ze, cutting his privilege of riding a horse (his favourite hobby) for a month. The next day he wrote a letter to us all asking for forgiveness, and from that moment on there was a dramatic change in his life and he never spoke about death and accidents or told morbid stories again.

The letter:

April 4th 1994
Dear Tios and Tias

Tios forgive me for the problems that I have caused since I've been here.

Tios forgive me for my mischievousness and for the bad things I have done. Because God has cleaned my heart even more now.

Please don't be angry with me because I don't want to fight with anyone any more.

God is with us and will protect us all. God has put lots of love in my heart for all the Tios and Tias here on the farm.
With lots of love,
Jose Roberto

When a child receives limits and discipline he feels loved and secure. The disciplines we give the children vary from case to case and have to be handled with wisdom. More often than not we cut their privileges (e.g. they can't go on an outing). In the heat of the moment we send the child to his room to cool off, which is followed by talking with him.

But however much we can give them physically and mentally, there is only one person who can change them from the inside and that's Jesus. Every morning for an hour they started to learn about the everlasting love of God, His abounding forgiveness which so many were hungry for, His loyalty and faithfulness, His desire to give them a new life, to be the Father they had never had. We were only channels between God and these children and teenagers, and without exception we the workers were and still are treated by Him the same as they are.

In March and April Mauro and Marcos, Jose Carlos and Alberto, two sets of brothers, and Marcello arrived on the farm. Mauro, thirteen, and Marcos, twelve, had different fathers. Mauro was short and skinny with undernourishment, he walked with a skip and liked wearing his straight brown hair long to cover his eyes. His skin was lily white. Marcos was taller with dark brown skin and a mass of thick dark hair. His fine features and big brown eyes were always screwed up in anger. Their mother, a prostitute, had walked out on them a year earlier and never returned. They'd gone to live with an aunt whose poverty-stricken home had rats living in it with her; apparently some were white and as large as cats. Both boys spent their time on the streets and not at school. Marcos couriered drugs for traffickers and Mauro played video games at the local bar all day.

'It was the only way I could forget my mother,' Mauro told me later.

They both had a deep hate for their mother. She'd rejected them without an explanation.

'I don't even like to think about her,' Marcos told me with anger in his eyes, 'I will never forgive her for leaving me.'

Marcos's anger and inability to forgive her made him temperamental and indifferent with everyone. He held grudges against any of the boys or workers who misunderstood him, and over-reacted in tantrums if teased, which delighted the boys and encouraged them all the more.

Marcello was seven years old. When he was four months, his mother, brother and sister drowned in a flooding river which flowed past their small grass hut. A woman from a neighbouring village found him dying of hunger the next day, along with his six other brothers and sisters. His father lived elsewhere. Dona Maria and her husband decided to adopt Marcello, even though they had ten children of their own. His tiny brown body was covered in open wounds, especially on his scalp, and he was desperately undernourished. However, with medication and good food his body weight soon normalised and by one year old, against all the odds, he was walking. But Marcello had given the elderly couple more problems than all their ten children put together, spending most of his time on the streets in rebellion. The couple, now in their late sixties, could not control him any more and called the Conselho Tutelar for help. After a week in the FEBEM, Fatima from the Tutelar begged us to take him at the farm. We agreed.

Jose Carlos, eleven, and Alberto, ten, had come from a violent home. The police had been called in by neighbours on numerous occasions to stop their father beating them all to death.

'I saw my father throw my mother against the wall once. She was pregnant at the time and lost the baby,' Alberto told me soon after he'd arrived.

Alberto wet his pants regularly throughout the day. Jose Carlos tried to act like a grown man. As the eldest he'd taken the role of protecting his mother. The father had

eventually left their mother and had another family elsewhere, but he would return on occasions, when drunk out
of his mind, to fight and terrify them all. Their mother had
a lover half her age and there wasn't room in her two-
roomed house for them all. The Conselho Tutelar asked
us, as a favour, to take in the boys for a month even
though they had never lived on the streets, while they
sorted things out between their mother and father. This
never happened, however, and the boys stayed on the farm
for a year and a half.

After two months on the farm Januario, the boy whose
crazed mother had locked him up for so long, had stopped
walking on all fours and was eating at the table. But
whenever he prayed, worshipped or sang to Jesus he
became restless and his body would start to contort. He
drew demon-like heads on every bit of paper he could lay
his hands on. We had also discovered that before being
shut in darkness for a year he had spent most of his time
at the local Macumba centre where he would drink the
wine and blood offered to the demons.

One morning in early April, Mags, a short-term missionary from the Salvation Army in England, complained that
Januario had growled at her with a contorted face and
clawed hands during meditation. That same evening at
the service, while Pastor Marcelino was speaking about
David fighting the giant Goliath with only a stone and a
sling, Januario started to become restless. He stood up
and came and sat next to me, his body twisting and
turning. Everyone had one eye on Januario and one eye on
the pastor, including the pastor. I immediately sensed an
evil presence and I felt myself shiver as I had when first

meeting Minerinho on the streets of Rio. Suddenly the same warmth of the Holy Spirit started rising within me and I began to pray. But the more I prayed the heavier I felt.

That night three of us workers had the same dream. And I am not one to have dreams. In the dream Januario was being persecuted by demons and he was doing evil things. Then suddenly a pastor appeared and said slowly and powerfully to Januario, 'Jesus Christ is the Son of God.' Januario turned around and with an expression of amazement he asked the pastor to repeat his words. Then in my dream I heard Jesus saying to me, 'In this case you will have to fast and pray, for there are legions.'

The next morning we all came together to pray. Pastor Marcelino had already had experience in deliverance and suggested that we specifically consecrate the following day to fasting and praying for Januario.

'Most of these evil spirits will not be able to stay for very much longer anyway because of the presence of God here, but for the others to leave we will need to pray and fast,' explained the Pastor, referring to Mark 9:29.

Januario liked his own sex and spent a lot of his spare time telling Ailton that he'd make a beautiful woman. He also refused to change his clothes and wore a thick orange-coloured jumper in the 30°C Brazilian sunshine, day after day. On a visit to their parents' dark and filthy home we had discovered a drunk father, who had apparently abused his sons sexually as children, a crazy mother who was still talking about the police throwing stones at her house, three dogs who were never let out to do what they had to do and a kitchen permanently filled with smoke from the old stove because a window was never opened. We'd started to pray for them too.

Also, Januario had recently cornered a visiting volunteer from the Lagoinha church and told the shocked young man that he knew the details of homosexual relationships he (the volunteer) had had before becoming a Christian. The young man was beside himself because he'd told no one after his conversion. When Ricardo confronted Januario as to how he knew, Januario said that he'd heard a voice telling him everything.

On the day of fasting and praying for Januario seven of us came together and, directed by the pastor, consecrated our lives to Jesus.

'Now let's hold hands and pray for protection over one another and over our families,' continued Marcelino. 'And then let's sing and exalt our Lord.'

Suddenly, while we were praising God, the room was filled with the powerful presence of the Holy Spirit and we started to intercede on behalf of Januario's life.

After half an hour we called for Januario to join us.

'Keep your eyes open while praying for him,' said the pastor.

He stood in the middle of us and we continued to pray, rebuking the demons one by one in the name and authority of Jesus Christ.

A few weeks later we felt directed by God to fast and pray once again. This time Januario renounced all the pacts he'd made with Satan. He asked Jesus to come into his life and to be his new Lord. He prayed for salvation, he prayed for a new beginning.

After this Januario's life completely turned around. He became more peaceful and was able to pray and sing in the presence of God. He stopped drawing demon-like heads. He threw his jumper away. Ailton was left in peace.

And for the first time in fourteen years Januario was able to go to school to learn how to read and write.

9

Families

'You will draw water from the wells of salvation,' said one woman to my right.

'I can see a jug of oil being broken and oil pouring out everywhere,' said another from behind me.

'I have received a word for you in Isaiah 41, verses 17 to 20.'

The poor and needy search for water, but there is none; their tongues are parched with thirst. But I the Lord will answer them; I, the God of Israel, will not forsake them. I will make rivers flow on barren heights, and springs within the valleys. I will turn the desert into pools of water, and the parched ground into springs. I will put in the desert the cedar and the acacia, the myrtle and the olive. I will set pines in the wasteland, the fir and the cypress together, so that people may see and know, may consider and understand, that the hand of the Lord has done this, that the Holy One of Israel has created it.

It was September 1994. I was in Holy Trinity Brompton during a short trip to England. A women's group were praying for the families of the street children following a talk I'd given to them about our work. What I was hearing was making the hairs on my arms stand on end. God was saying that He was going to do miracles among the families of the children '... I will turn the desert into pools of water ... I will put in the desert the cedar and the acacia ...' This was the heart of God. He wanted to see broken families reunited. He wanted the mothers, fathers, grandmothers, grandfathers, aunts, uncles, brothers and sisters of these children to know He loved them. He wanted to take them out of their misery and give them a new purpose for living. He wanted to see them working, not unemployed and starving. He wanted to see them sober, not drunk so as to escape their reality. He wanted to see them in homes with running water, electricity and sewage systems. He wanted to see them sleeping in beds with blankets and not on the cold mud floor, naked. He wanted to give them back what the locusts had eaten, and He could do this because His Son Jesus had died for each one, had risen for each one and was alive for each one to be reunited with Him. If God was changing the lives of the children in the Centre and on the farm then He wanted to change the lives of their families, too.

But we had to do it God's way and not our way. The poverty was severe for many of these families and the tendency was to think that the only way to help them was to take them out of the favelas and give them new homes, food every day, take them physically to find a job. There was no question that one could contribute towards these things, and we were, but the danger was to create paternalism and dependency rather than motivating them to study and find jobs to earn money to better their homes and buy food and clothes, thereby creating independence. They also needed emotional help. If a mother had rejected her difficult son, her heart had to be changed. If she had been badly abused by her husband then she too needed inner healing. If the father was an alcoholic he was also looking for help, love and acceptance. If he was trafficking drugs, had other women and beat his wife he needed help, he was lost and empty inside. And there was only one person who could change them from the inside and that was Jesus Christ.

Instead of taking them out of the shantytowns we had to work at taking the shantytowns from their hearts; the misery, poor-mindedness, narrow vision of the world, low self-esteem, twisted perspectives, contorted view of the value that God has for them. A caterpillar crawls along the ground, destroying leaves, and has a limited perspective of the world around him. But when God changes him into a butterfly not only is he transformed physically to everyone around him, but his own perspective has changed. He is, however, in exactly the same context.

As a caterpillar is released from the ground to which he has been bound, so when Jesus comes into people's lives they are released from deep hurts, low self-image, worries about the future and their health.

The problem seemed too big to even try to contemplate a solution. In that year alone we had assisted around two hundred and twenty boys and girls in the day-care centre and more than forty of these had returned to live with their families. Many others had been referred on to other organisations and homes and thirty boys had gone on to the farm. That meant an awful lot of families needed following up, discipleship and care. Aside from a team of five part-time Christian psychologists, led and instructed by Silvia, who gave therapy to families three days a week in the Centre, we did not have the structure to do this effectively.

The families had to be visited in the favelas. Meanwhile, that August while I was praying God had given me a plan that was simple but would prove extremely effective. Every favela was based in a *bairro* (district/suburb) throughout the city and every biarro had its own local churches. If we could refer the families to discipleship home groups from a local church, ideally within or around the favela, that would welcome the families in and nurture them, thus enabling us to solve a large part of the problem. In other words, we would serve as the 'middlemen'.

This plan, however, would take a year to come into fruition.

A week before leaving for England I had made a visit to Carlos's house in Palmital, a large and desperately poor favela north of the city. It was a visit that would be hard to forget. Carlos was fourteen years old when he arrived on the farm in June. I'd first set eyes on him in the Casa Aberta which he frequented for a month before being referred on. One of the reasons he stood out was because he'd had his right eye pierced on the streets by the Marcia gang a few weeks earlier.

'One night they circled me,' he told me later. 'When I turned around a fat boy, a really big guy, hit me in the eye with one of those long fluorescent light bulbs.' He stayed in hospital for ten days but the doctors couldn't save his sight.

Carlos had seven brothers and sisters. Six were by the same father, who had eventually left them all for another woman, and the seventh, four-year-old Agatha, was by his mother's young boyfriend, Rogerio, who lived with her. Elizabete had managed to palm most of her children off into various institutions and orphanages; the rest were on the streets apart from Agatha and Darlan, her youngest son of seven years old. Carlos would talk constantly about Darlan, saying that he was left alone for sometimes three days in a row without food or water while Elizabete and Rogerio, with Agatha, went off on their various trips in an old van that constantly needed repairing. Carlos was angry with his mother and her boyfriend. She was tough, so he said, and they both had made him sleep outside in the *quintal* (back yard) while they slept in a double bed with Agatha.

'We have to go and help him, Sarah,' pleaded Carlos.

It was midday and the heat was intense. Marcia, a teacher at the farm, had joined me on the visit and we both kept begging Carlos to slow down as he ran on ahead of us up the side of the mountain towards his house, which was at the very top. Four months of no rain had made everything dry and the ground we walked on was pure red dust. Carlos had suggested that I park the car outside a bar at the bottom of the mountain, where the owner could watch it for us.

'It's a shady district round here,' Carlos had said with a grin.

Mountains circled the valley as far as the eye could see, each one covered in hundreds of tiny matchbox houses surrounded by the dry red earth; there was no grass or tree in sight. Over in the distance beyond the mountains loomed the skyscrapers of downtown Belo Horizonte. The majority of these inhabitants had no running water or sewage systems. Water had to be carried up the mountain by hand in buckets and pans from a well in the valley.

We eventually came to a ridge in the path before climbing an even steeper and dustier path to the houses on the very top.

'How does anyone manage to climb up here in the rainy season?' puffed an unfit Marcia. 'This dust must turn into pure mud.'

'It's virtually impossible,' shouted back Carlos, who was at the top already.

'I need a drink of water desperately before going on,' gasped Marcia.

A young couple came to Marcia's rescue while Carlos ran on ahead to see if anyone was at home. They knew Elizabete and confirmed that Darlan was left alone for days at a time with no food or water.

'He runs around the neighbours, begging for food,' said the young man. 'Only last week he fainted. Don't ask me where they go on these trips but they leave him behind.' Carlos returned saying that his mother and Rogerio were out but that Darlan was there, all alone once again.

We quickly said our goodbyes and followed Carlos. A little black figure was curled up on top of an old broken yellow cooker in the quintal which ran along the outside of the small one-room brick house. It was fenced with broken bits of wooden planks, and black plastic covered the roof area above our heads. Darlan was looking out through a hole in a plank at the valley below.

'I'm waiting for my mother and Rogerio to return,' said Darlan feebly.

Marcia pointed to some bits of plastic and a couple of empty bottles that were arranged in a circle on the dusty floor. They were Darlan's only toys.

'How long has she been away?' asked Carlos, concerned.

'She left this morning. I don't know if they will be back tonight. She left me some rice in a pan, only I ate that for lunch,' he said, indicating an old-fashioned iron stove opposite him. I noticed that the old stove was heated by bits of wood and pieces of newspaper. Next to the stove was a curtained area where they washed. It was the size of a small cubicle, but there was no such luxury as a shower with running hot and cold water. Darlan's bed was between the tiny cubicle and the door to the brick room, which was padlocked. His bed consisted of a blanket on the bare earth.

'My mother always padlocks the door when they leave,' Darlan informed us.

'They sleep on a double bed with a mattress, sheets and blankets,' continued Carlos bitterly. 'They also have a TV in there.'

'It's all right for you now, Carlos, you have somewhere to live where people love you and take care of you,' said Darlan sadly. 'I'm here all alone carrying water every day up the mountainside for them. When I'm alone I feel scared at night, and sometimes the light goes out.' He pointed to a single light bulb dangling dangerously and vulnerably down from the plastic roof above us.

I noticed that Marcia's eyes had filled with tears and Carlos was looking at his feet. Swallowing the lump in my throat I tried desperately to get control of myself.

'Carlos,' I said quickly, 'pray and ask God to give you a verse in the Bible especially for Darlan.'

Carlos prayed and suddenly he said, 'Wow, as clear as anything Psalm 3 verse 3 came into my mind. That's never happened to me before, and I haven't got a clue what it says.'

'So open your Bible and have a look,' I said expectantly.

Carlos fumbled to open his Bible and read slowly, 'But you are a shield around me, O Lord; you bestow glory on me and lift up my head.'

Darlan's face broke into a big white smile.

'That's amazing,' laughed Carlos with joy. 'That's from God, Darlan. You are never alone here because Jesus is here with you, protecting you. Don't be afraid.'

We all walked down the mountainside together, and getting into the boiling hot car drove to the supermarket to buy Darlan some food. Before saying goodbye, however, I told Darlan to tell his mother that she had to stay in her house all day Saturday, which was in two days' time, because I would be returning with the Conselho Tutelar. Elizabete needed to answer some questions. And I wanted to talk to Joao about taking Darlan to the farm in Ravena. Although he wasn't on the streets, his case was an emergency.

That Saturday Elizabete was waiting for us. The small room was no longer padlocked and we were ushered in and invited to sit on her double bed. A Bible was opened and purposely placed where we'd see it. A large black lady with a forceful personality, Elizabete was soon on the defensive with the presence of the Conselho Tutelar and flatly denied ever leaving Darlan alone at night or for days without food.

'Your neighbours confirm otherwise, and we are concerned about the welfare of your son,' I explained firmly.

Elizabete readily consented to let Darlan go with us to the farm. We arranged to visit her soon, together with her two sons. Elizabete needed firm encouragement to find work once again, for which she was very capable, in order

to improve their living conditions and to re-assume
motherhood for her many abandoned children. An ex-
Macumbeira (practitioner of spiritism), she was also lack-
ing direction spiritually. Apparently she had stopped prac-
tising spiritism because her life had started to fall apart:
losing her job, husband, home and children.

Meanwhile, within a few weeks on the farm Darlan's
health improved and he started to put on weight.

Every Friday night the boys on the farm have a time of
intercession together with the team. It is important that
they understand that through the many difficulties which
we at Crianca Feliz encounter in our efforts to help them,
we are all dependent on God. It is a faith-building experience for everyone, and prayers are answered sometimes
within only a few days: Ze's mother became a Christian;
we received $US23,000 from Brazilian supporters to buy a
BESTA Kia twelve-seater mini-bus, and even the last
$US1,400 we required to pay for the insurance arrived
anonymously from someone at Holy Trinity Brompton in
London with a note saying 'Specifically for the BESTA!';
after five months of drought, Juarez asked God to send
rain that night and it poured down, filling the empty tanks
to the top; the boys prayed for one another and for their
friends and brothers and sisters still living on the streets;
they learned how to forgive their mothers and fathers; we
received donations of clothes, trainers, bicycles, toys; members of the Full Gospel Businessmen's Fellowship with
shops in CEASA (equivalent to Covent Garden fruit and
vegetable market in London) offered to give us a vanload
of fresh produce every Friday morning. Over and over
again we were able to thank God for answering our

prayers from one week to the next, and the faith of the boys as well as the workers grew in leaps and bounds.

Along with Carlos and Darlan, nine other boys had arrived on the farm: Juarez, Julio, Anderson, Derson, Wender and Washington from the Casa Aberta, Edson and Wallace through the Conselho Tutelar and Samuel from the restoration house. Wallace, aged nine, had had his life threatened by a gang who were using him to break into houses because of his small size. He lived in an enormous favela called Jardim de Felicidade, meaning Garden of Happiness, which couldn't have been further from the truth. He lived with his mother and two sisters in a tiny one-room house by the side of a thin running river full of waste. There was often shooting at night, and during the day while his mother worked he ran to the streets with the gang. He later told me, 'The boys were big and I was small. What they ordered me to do I had to obey, otherwise they beat me.'

Edson was labelled 'impossible' and 'a thief' by his neighbourhood. The judge in General Carneiro, Sabara, where he lived did not know what to do with him and someone suggested he be sent to us for a month. That month turned into months. Edson's nervous and hyperactive disposition was made worse by the severe beatings he'd received from his aggressive father. Edson had got into a bad crowd and become one of the worst of them and his mother couldn't cope. His father had other women with children and would return home occasionally to sleep with his mother. She only put up with this because he still paid the bills. Edson, fifteen, tall and blond-haired, found his forte when he arrived at the farm. He needed the wide

155

open spaces into which he could channel his excess energy and eventually became one of the best workers on the land.

Washington, twelve, and Juarez, ten, were brothers. They had different fathers, and their mother drank excessively. When Washington was two years old she would tie him to the bed and go out leaving him alone all day long. The boys were permanently hungry as she spent all her money and time in the local bar. Eventually their mother died of alcoholic poisoning and Juarez and Washington made the streets their home.

Julio was black with a large head and an even larger smile. He was ten years old and had ten brothers and sisters. He lived in Sao Lucas, a favela in central Belo, in a filthy house made of thin planks of wood with no windows. His parents were separated, and he hadn't seen his father for years. When his mother went out to work his older brothers would beat him up until eventually he could take no more and ran to the streets. 'At night it was cold and sometimes it would start to rain. I couldn't sleep until the early hours of the morning,' Julio told me. 'I was filthy too and smelt bad. Twice I was nearly raped.'

Anderson was twelve years old. Skinny with fair skin and fair hair in tight curls, Anderson was gifted in everything he did: football, music, school. He was born in Bahia, north Brazil. His mother brought him south to Belo Horizonte when he was only a baby and married his stepfather with whom she had another four children. His stepfather, however, didn't like him because he wasn't his son and they fought constantly. 'Once he tried to kill my mother. He had another woman and my mother sent him out of the house. One day he came back and attacked her with a knife,' Anderson told me later. 'I ran away to the streets and stayed with Julio [they were neighbours in Sao Lucas] and others for almost a year.'

Samuel had lived in Youth With A Mission's restoration house for a year and a half and had asked if he could come and live on the farm with us. He was supposedly restored and it was time for him to work, so Joao gave him the job of starting a large vegetable garden on the land. Samuel was sixteen years old and lazy. He was to cause us as much work initially as all the other boys put together, and it took a great effort to get him to even water the garden, let alone weed it! After a year on the farm Helio Valadao, the brother of Pastor Marcio with a large bakery franchise, gave Samuel the opportunity to train as a baker and to work in one of the shops.

Derson lived in miserable conditions. His father had died, leaving his mother with seven children, and they all lived together in a one-room house in Teresopolis. 'One day I ran away from home alone,' Derson told me. 'I hid alone and started to sleep. But it started to rain and I felt really cold. Then a lady gave me a blanket and I slept.' He eventually went to the Casa Aberta and was referred on to the farm. Black with a bright expressive face, Derson liked to be the clown and to make everyone laugh, only underneath this front he was hurting. During the first therapy session with his mother he cried for over an hour.

Wender was eight years old when he arrived on the farm. He had four brothers and one sister, all of whom lived with neighbours in Palmital. 'I didn't like to stay at home because my mother left us on our own often. I never knew my father. My home has one room only, it is tiny and has no water or toilet,' Wender told me. 'When I was eight years old I took the bus into the city. At night we put plastic on the ground because it was so cold.' Together with Derson he went to the Casa Aberta.

His best friend on the farm is Lucas, my son.

In March 1994 we had opened the first of our three 'family foster homes'. This was part of our planned third stage in the programme and was for the children who were already restored but who had no possibility of returning to live with their own parents. The homes were to be run by Christian couples who not only felt called by God to foster these children, but who had previous experience working with them. Crianca Feliz would help finance the running of the house including rent, if necessary, extra furniture, equipment for the kitchen and laundry, school books, clothes and so on, and Silvia and her team would provide monthly family therapy sessions to iron out any problems that surfaced. The first couple took in Giselle and Marcos Silva and they proposed to take in two others within the following six months. The man had been one of these boys himself and had been brought up in a Christian home run by a Canadian missionary couple working in Belo Horizonte. Now older, married and a father himself, he wanted to do the same for other boys. His wife professed to be 100 per cent behind him.

The other two homes opened in July of the same year. One couple took in Eduardo and Cristiano; the man was a pastor for a small church in Contagem and his wife had worked in the Casa Aberta. They had their own baby son. The other couple took in Joao Carlos, Kleber and Samuel. The man worked for the local council of Sabara, and he and his wife had been helping needy teenagers since they married ten years earlier. They had two young children of their own.

Within six or seven months of opening these homes, however, each one of them closed. The first couple kept Giselle and sent back Marcos Silva, saying they didn't want any more children, because the wife wasn't prepared to have an extended family after all. Eduardo and Cristiano ran away from the second house. The pastor couldn't cope and had started to over-discipline the boys. They in turn revolted against him and went back to their parents in the favela, but within weeks Eduardo was back on the streets. We had to close the third house when we discovered that the money we were giving to the couple towards the upkeep of the boys was being used elsewhere.

It thus became very clear very quickly that 'family foster homes' were not going to be the immediate answer for these boys.

'What you need,' said our adviser Pastor Marcio from the Lagoinha church, 'is a family who will foster one child into their own home, but without any financial support from the ministry. It's the family who take the child on and who support him. Otherwise you will have problems that you do not need.'

Also, once again, God was showing us that the priority in each child's life was their own family. If they couldn't return to live with their parents then if possible the next best thing, before a foster family, was a relative, be it a grandmother, aunt, uncle, brother or sister. In April of the following year Marcos Silva went to live with his grandmother in the interior of Minas Gerais. It was an answer to his prayers.

The second thing we had on our hearts were *Casa*

Republicas, houses or apartments in the city where up to six teenagers, together with two workers from the ministry, could live. These teenagers from the farm would be restored, working and studying in the city and would help towards paying rent and the bills. In other words, we would be making them independent. The following September we opened our first Casa Republica.

In October Fernando Henrique was elected President of Brazil. His unanimous win was partly encouraged by his instigation of the country's new currency, the Real dollar, five months before the elections. Inflation had dropped dramatically from 46 per cent per month to 4 per cent per month, and on the day he was made President the Real dollar was stronger than the US dollar.

For Christmas 1994 Holy Trinity Brompton sent their second team that year. Caroline Taylor, who had become the co-ordinator for Happy Child in England, led the team once again. News about the Toronto Blessing had filtered through and we were all expectant to see what God would do through this small team of four people during their month with us.

At the beginning of that year in a small Vineyard church at the end of the airport runway in Toronto, Canada, the most extraordinary outpouring of God's Holy Spirit had occurred. Within eighteen weeks, over a quarter of a million people from churches around the world had been to Toronto to see and receive all that God had for them. At the end of May Elli Mumford, co-leader with her husband of the South West London Vineyard Church, spoke in Holy Trinity Brompton on what she had seen in Toronto.

'The power of God was poured out in incredible measure, just like the Bible talks about in the book of Acts, chapters two and four. We saw everything save tongues of fire. It was all accompanied by phenomena. But the phenomena are very secondary, the whole move of the Lord is only about Jesus. It's all happened before. This is just the refreshing of the Spirit of God. It talks in the book of Acts about times of refreshing from the Spirit of the Lord and that is what God is doing. He's pouring His Spirit out upon us, He's sending us His joy and refreshing our spirits just because He loves us.'

She went on to pray for the church that day and the same outpouring of God's Holy Spirit happened there too: broken marriages were healed; demoralised pastors were refreshed; the deaf could hear; people's relationships with Jesus were transformed.

Eventually the whole Church throughout England was affected.

Early one morning during the team's first week with us Joao mentioned to me that they were praying with the boys in the *Galpao* (Warehouse) and that they might need my help. I will never forget walking into the room in the Warehouse to find twenty-three children and teenagers on the floor, 'slain' by the Holy Spirit. Sally, one of the members of the team who was praying over Marcello, looked up at me and smiled with a shrug of the shoulders. Some were laughing, others were crying, some were shaking, and the presence of God was powerful. Oades and Julio, who had been prayed for and were now on their feet, came rushing over, saying they wanted to pray for me. I was tired, demoralised, two months pregnant with my second child and needing refreshment desperately. I agreed. As they started to pray for me I suddenly felt a warming heat rushing right through me, as though my entire being was being embraced by God's tremendous love. Before I knew it someone had caught me from behind and I was flat on my back. Fully conscious and yet unable to move as wave upon wave of the Holy Spirit rushed through me, I could hear Oades praying with a sensitivity and a precision that made me start to weep. These children who months earlier had been on the streets with no love, direction or future were now transformed through the knowledge of God's love for them, and now they were praying for me!

Suddenly into my thoughts as clear as can be I heard God's voice saying, 'Thank you, thank you for obeying Me.' All sense of despair, homesickness for my family in England and exhaustion disappeared as I recommitted myself once again to God's purpose.

Personal testimonies of the lives of some of these boys are written in chapter 12 of this book. However, here are a few extracts of what God did in some of their lives that day:

Welbert: 'When they prayed for me, once again I felt this incredible joy flooding my body. Then I had a vision and I saw an arm extending out towards me, and I cried out loud, "I want to go, I want to go." And then I heard a voice saying to me, "No, it's not the right time yet, but I will use you in my work in the future." It was Jesus.'

Carlos: 'When I received the Holy Spirit, for the first time in my life I saw a vision. God showed me that angels were working on my heart. It was like seeing a spiritual oper-ation. After this I really started to pray.'

Anderson: 'When I was prayed for I saw a picture of clouds and Jesus was there waiting for me. I will never forget this moment, it is deep in my heart.'

Oades: 'I started to shake and cry. Then I stopped crying and started to laugh and laugh. Suddenly I saw in my mind a picture of what I thought was heaven. It was a place full of clouds and beautiful trees and birds. There were lakes, waterfalls and animals. And as I was walking through this place I crossed over into what seemed to be hell. Every-thing was red and the trees were dead. The place with a waterfall was the same as I'd seen in heaven, only the water was blood. I heard people screaming. I had pre-viously asked God to show me what heaven and hell looked like, so this was an answer to my prayer.'

Januario: 'I saw a picture and a demon was speaking to me, tormenting me and I was shaking with fear. Then Jesus arrived and spoke to me saying that I didn't have to fear the bad things but that I should have faith in the word of God.'

Derson: 'I saw a picture of heaven with Jesus and His disciples; they were all white and looked like angels. Heaven is very beautiful.'

God had told Marcos, the brother of Mauro, that he could forgive his mother. This was still a very sensitive subject and he continued to be highly temperamental and difficult.

Then two months later during meditation Mauro told me that he'd had a dream that his mother, whom they hadn't seen or heard from since she'd walked out of their house two years earlier, had come to visit them on the farm. That afternoon the Conselho Tutelar called Joao to say that Gleice, Mauro and Marcos's mother, had been in contact and wanted to visit her two sons!

The following week, without any warning, she turned up at the farm. The two brothers were still at school and it gave us time to talk to her while one of the workers, also called Mauro, went on ahead to the school to prepare them.

'The best thing you can do, Gleice, is to ask forgiveness from them both for leaving them,' I explained gently.

'Oh no, no, no,' answered Gleice, shaking her head and looking down at her feet. 'I've already asked forgiveness from God and that's enough.' She was small and fair-skinned with a mass of tight, curly dark hair. Her face showed clearly that she'd suffered in her thirty-odd years. She was currently living in Rio de Janeiro with her new boyfriend and was no longer working as a prostitute. Her obvious nervousness grew more pronounced as she waited for her sons to arrive.

'Gleice,' said Marcia firmly, 'Marcos has been badly affected by what happened. He feels anger towards you for rejecting him, and this has caused us a lot of problems because he transfers this anger on others around him. Mauro, on the other hand, has managed to forgive you.'

'No, you're mistaken,' continued Gleice, 'Mauro is the difficult one, not Marcos.'

'Well, I think we had better warn you that Marcos feels very badly towards you, Gleice, and even though you've

164

asked forgiveness from God you must ask for forgiveness personally from the people you've hurt. Otherwise your sons will never be freed from the deep hurt and anger they are holding on to,' I said emphatically.

I went on ahead to speak to the boys who had arrived from school and were waiting on the veranda next to my house. They were both sitting down, nervously looking at their feet. Marcos's face was closed and full of anger as a thousand thoughts went through his mind. O God, I prayed inside, please make this reunion a time of healing for all three of them.

Suddenly Gleice appeared around the side of the house. As soon as she saw them she stopped and bowed her head. Overcome with emotion, she burst into tears as she continued to walk slowly towards them. Marcos didn't take his eyes from the floor and Mauro looked at her, not knowing what to do next.

'Go and give your mother a hug,' I suggested, swallowing a lump in my throat.

Mauro stood up and hugged his mother, bursting into tears as he did so.

'I'm sorry, so sorry for leaving you, please forgive me,' she said through loud sobs.

I looked at Marcos. He was still looking at the floor with a tight, screwed-up face, only big tears had started to roll down his cheeks.

'I forgive you,' sobbed Mauro as he kept holding on to his mother.

'Marcos,' she said, hurt, 'Forgive me, please forgive me, don't hold on to your anger. I'm so sorry for what I did.'

Tears continued to flow down his cheeks, but he couldn't bring himself to embrace her or to forgive her. I could almost feel the terrible turmoil he was in. All those sleepless nights planning how he would scream at her for rejecting him, how he would never ever forgive her. And now, after two years, there she was before him in person, saying she was sorry.

Mauro wanted to show her his school books which were in his bedroom. But Gleice was concerned about Marcos. I told her to go on ahead while I spoke to him.

'Your mother was wrong to leave you, Marcos, and I understand that it hurt you very deeply,' I said as soon as they'd left. 'It must be difficult to forgive her. But she's here in person asking you for forgiveness, and you must forgive her, Marcos, you must. It is difficult, and it's normal to feel the way you do, but don't miss this opportunity to forgive her.'

Marcos said nothing as we walked up the hill to Mauro's bedroom. As soon as Gleice saw Marcos coming she ran to him and embraced him. Then ever so slightly I saw Marcos respond with his arms, and I knew immediately that he'd let go of the anger that he'd held on to for so long.

From that day on Marcos started to change, and a week later he managed to forgive everyone he'd held a grudge against. Gleice stayed in contact and sent them both some money and a card for their birthdays. Although it would take time for his temperament to adjust, the real Marcos started to shine. He is now a happy, sensitive and friendly teenager.

The Night Shelter:
'On the Road to Emmaus . . .'

'What's happened?' I asked, concerned.

'It's Rodrigo, he's had an accident in the new BESTA mini-bus,' answered Joao white-faced as he ran into the house.

'Where? Is anyone hurt?' I asked, all at once.

'He crashed on the main road to the farm from the city. Ricardo and I are going there now. Thank God there were no children with him.'

The mini-bus was a complete write-off. He had been driving very fast around a bend on one of the most dangerous stretches of the BR262, lost control, shot across the opposite side of the road, hit a rock and flown three metres before smashing to the ground upside-down. Rodrigo had escaped with a broken finger and some cuts and bruises.

But there was worse to come. When the federal police arrived on the scene they took one look at Rodrigo's driver's licence and announced that it was false; it had been bought in Rio de Janeiro. Joao was gobsmacked. Rodrigo, a retired fireman and member of an evangelical church, had assured Joao that his licence was clean and valid and that he'd driven a mini-bus for twenty years. What's more, his wife, who had been working in the Casa

Aberta for three months, confirmed that all he'd said was true. And Ricardo had taken him on a test drive and given him the all clear a week earlier.

The federal policeman took Joao and Ricardo aside and explained that the insurance company would not pay for a new mini-bus because the licence was false, but that he was very sympathetic with the work we did for the children. What he could do was to write on the statement that the driver had been Ricardo, whose licence was clean, and so the insurance company would pay. He encouraged them by saying that he understood that they were Christians but that they should do it for the children – they needed a mini-bus, after all.

Joao was handed a big temptation on a large silver plate. A hundred thoughts rushed through his mind. But eventually he said, 'I understand that you want to help us, but we bought this mini-bus with a lot of sacrifice and clean money and it is used for the work of God. If God gave one mini-bus He can give us another ten if He wants to. I won't negotiate with my treasure in heaven by lying to insurance companies. I would prefer to lose the mini-bus than lie.'

The federal policeman persisted, however, and told Joao to think about it for three days. I too was adamant that we speak the truth and Joao returned three days later to confirm his original position. Sure enough, the insurance company declared that under the circumstances our cover was void. We'd been robbed of the vehicle we'd been given after months and months of prayer. Everyone felt terrible, especially Rodrigo who asked us to forgive him for having lied about the driving licence.

On January 15th 1995, ten days after the accident, a

new head of the claims department was appointed at the company. He just happened to be a Christian and a member of the Lagoinha church. After a meeting with Joao, he proclaimed, 'Look, you only have a one per cent chance of reclaiming the total loss. But let's work on that one per cent chance, put it in God's hands because He is the Lord. Write a full report describing the whole situation and I will present it to the committee. Keep praying and fasting.'

Two months later, during a team prayer meeting at the farm one Saturday, God spoke to us specifically about the mini-bus. One person saw a picture in their mind of a large red mini-bus with wings coming down from heaven. Another person saw a smaller pink mini-bus. And yet another saw the numbers 7,7,7.

Immediately Joao said, 'God is saying that He is going to give us two new mini-buses, one larger than the other. And seven plus seven plus seven makes twenty-one. The insurance company are going to release us money after all and it will be $21,000 Reais!'

The following Monday, in faith, Joao went to put a down-payment on an eighteen-seater red Topic ASIA mini-bus costing $26,000 Reais, using the $10,000 Reais we had saved towards buying the farm, should the possibility arise. The sales assistant told Joao that the price was going up 12 per cent the following day and that he had forty-eight hours to pay the remaining $16,000 Reais.

On Tuesday morning we received a fax from the insurance company saying that against all the odds they had agreed to pay $16,500 Reais towards a new mini-bus. We were all overjoyed, our prayers had been answered. But Joao wasn't celebrating.

'God told us $21,000 Reais, not $16,500. I'm going there now to speak to them,' he said emphatically.

We were all aghast at his reaction, but everyone including the boys on the farm got together to pray.

During Joao's meeting with the claims department they said on the spot that they'd pay an extra $2,500 Reais. But Joao insisted, saying that the original BESTA was valued at $23,000 Reais.

That afternoon we received another fax at the farm from the company. They'd agreed to pay $21,000 Reais!

Joao paid the remaining $16,000 on the Topic and put a down-payment on a second mini-bus, another twelve-seater BESTA Kia, which we received four months later. It was pink.

If we honour God, He will honour us.

On March 23rd we opened the night shelter. After nine months of praying and searching we eventually found a house large enough to sleep twelve to sixteen children and six workers. Situated in the smart and spacious *bairro* (suburb) of Pampulha to the north east of the city centre, the house had six large bedrooms, five bathrooms, two enormous reception rooms, a large kitchen and laundry room. A swimming pool at the back of the house took up almost the whole garden space and there were no close neighbours, which was to our advantage because there would be no complaints.

The shelter was the missing link in our programme. The children attending the Casa Aberta were returning to the streets at night, and this made our work less effective. Also the shelter would help towards the work we were doing at the farm. It would allow us more time to locate and work with the family of each boy, while the boys themselves were off the streets and in the shelter. After a month of recuperation some of the boys would not even need to go to the farm and could return directly to live with their families. However, those needing more restoration after that month, and whose families were still unprepared or unable to receive them back, could go to live on the farm but with a sounder basis of preparation.

The relatively few street girls who attended the Casa Aberta stayed in a night shelter and in restoration houses run by the Prefeitura and Youth With A Mission.

We invited Marcia to lead the shelter. She had been working with the ministry for over a year, was a mature woman in her mid-thirties and had been working in missions for many years. During a time of prayer for the shelter she read in Luke, chapter 24, verses 13 to 35, about when Jesus, after His resurrection, joined two of the disciples on the road to Emmaus, a village outside Jerusalem. When they arrived the two disciples invited Jesus to eat dinner and stay the night with them. And while at the table Jesus took the bread, gave thanks, and broke it in half and began to give it to them. It was then that their eyes were opened and they recognised Him.

Marcia shared this with Joao and me, adding, 'I think we should call the night shelter Casa Emmaus, because it is a place where the children too will find rest for their weary heads, a place where they will find love, comfort and security. When Jesus stayed in Emmaus He was resurrected, and this house will be a place where death is turned into life.'

Joao later discovered that in 1099 some Crusaders found the remains of a Roman castle called Castellum Emmaus, in what was most probably the original location of the village itself outside Jerusalem.

The Prefeitura signed a year's contract to help finance the running of the shelter, which they'd previously done for the Casa Aberta a year earlier. However, their bureaucratic system provided endless paperwork and monthly payments did not always arrive on time, sometimes coming two or three months late. Compassion International continued to renew their yearly contract which was now used to help run the work on the farm.

God uses the financially difficult times to remind us all who we are working for and why. The work is tiring, it uses all of you and if we didn't have that love from God constantly renewed then we couldn't persevere. If the work is God's then why should we ever have to close the ministry through lack of money? The financially difficult times were and still are used again and again to bring us all together as a team and to pray, pray, pray. They are times when we look at ourselves and our motives, they are times when we remind ourselves that we depend on God 100 per cent. Over and over again we see His provision, both in our personal needs and in the ministry. At the Casa Aberta the local bakery committed themselves to giving bread free every day. Churches give large *Cesta Basicas* (boxes full of the basic foods such as rice, beans, sugar, flour, coffee) which in turn we can give to the families. One day a pizza restaurant even donated around two thousand four hundred egg yolks to the farm!

Offerings from abroad arrive just at the right time, enabling us to buy meat and chicken, to buy medication for the children, to pay for school books, to pay the rent for the shelter.

*

After opening Casa Emmaus, the first four months were to prove the most difficult, as we established the schedule and a good working team. Anderson was leading the street work and it was essential that he lived in the shelter initially, together with Dora who was also a member of his street team. They knew the street children in 'their world' and the children knew them. Ruth, from England, who had been with another mission working with children in north Brazil, also joined the team, as did Thea from Holland, who had been working with Youth With A Mission.

One Saturday night during the first month, there were eight children in the shelter and they were in the sitting room watching television. Marcia was in her room when all at once the house felt very quiet. She quickly came out and went into the sitting room to be told to her horror that six boys had suddenly left the house. A news report had shown a party happening on the streets of the city centre; one of the boys had seen his street friends on the television and decided to run away to the party, taking five others with him. The workers immediately ran after them to see if they could find them, but returned at midnight with no children. After a time of prayer Marcia heard God telling her that all six of them would come back. Sure enough, at 2.30 a.m. the doorbell rang and when she opened the door she found six little faces staring at her. Everyone was overjoyed but it was a lesson sorely learned.

By early July relationships between the two teams at the Casa Aberta and Casa Emmaus were poor. There were criticisms of leadership, schedules and the way the boys were acting after a night in the shelter. There were negative comments about lack of workers in the shelter and having to take the boys to and from the centre on the bus, morning and night, Monday to Friday. The latter was understandable because the journey took over an hour, depending on the traffic, and street children at the best of times are not easy to control when all together. But attitudes were wrong. The extraordinary thing was that we'd had the second BESTA mini-bus for a few weeks but could not find a driver. This mini-bus was to be used in the city.

Eventually, Joao and I called a meeting between the two teams and gave everyone a chance to *lavar roupas sujos* (wash our dirty clothes).

'It is like a new marriage and at the moment the two sides are needing counselling,' explained Joao, breaking the ice and making everyone laugh. 'These two houses have to work well together because you are all working with the same children during the day and at night. God needs unity between you all if His work is going to be done properly, and if these children's lives are going to be changed.'

After two hours of confessing grudges, misunderstandings, dislikes and bad feelings, asking for forgiveness and forgiving, sharing suggestions and making amendments, I eventually shared two verses that God had given me that morning while praying for the meeting.

My eyes fail from weeping. I am in torment within, my heart is poured out on the ground because my people are destroyed, because children and infants faint in the streets of the city ... Arise, cry out in the night, as the watches of the night begin: pour out your heart like water in the presence of the Lord. Lift up your hands to

him for the lives of your children, who faint from hunger
at the head of every street. (Lam. 2:11,19)

'Let's keep our eyes focused on God's heart for these
children,' I continued. 'We are all here because He called
us to help rescue them from the dangerous streets they
have had to make their home. It's a sacrifice every day, but
it's worth it. Just to see these children once they're off the
streets, playing on the farm, studying, and eventually
working; happy and not sad, fed and not hungry, secure
and not frightened, and each with a personal knowledge
of the love Jesus has for them, makes it worth it. When I
take my eyes from God's heart and start to look at
everything and everyone working around me I start to
become critical, my attitude becomes negative and I feel
sorry for myself. If we have to take the children by bus
every day, it's a sacrifice, but it's the least we can do if it
means they won't have to spend a night on the streets.
Let's lift up our hands to God for the lives of these
children.'

At the end of the meeting we all had a time worshipping
the Lord together and there was the most wonderful sense
of unity, of God's presence with us, of His love, of being a
team working together to bring justice for those suffering
injustice. Two weeks later we found a motorist, Jorge, to
drive the mini-bus in the city, and the team in the shelter
started to increase. Kevin from the USA who had co-led
the restoration house at Youth With A Mission joined to
lead the visits to the families of the children in Casa
Emmaus; Milton also joined from the Renewed Baptist
church in Sabara, as did Henk from Brussels in Belgium.

After two years of operating, the Casa Aberta had

established an excellent daily schedule for the children and the team was well structured. The schedule now included sports twice weekly with a trained coach, a course teaching reading and writing, hygiene, art and painting with Denisia and Alessandra, and a trip to the park once a week. Dilma now assisted in the co-ordination of the activities in the centre allowing Selma more time to concentrate on administration. Vitor assisted Kevin and Milton to visit the families. Marcos chased after the documents of each child, found schools for them to study, helped locate families and took the children to the doctor and dentist. Cida and Alessandra taught songs and biblical stories illustrating the love of Jesus.

At four o'clock in the afternoons the children left the Casa Aberta to arrive at Casa Emmaus at five o'clock. Once in the shelter they would all jump in the pool for an hour, and after a shower and dinner would play games before going to bed. The team would pray for each one of the boys until they were calm and ready to sleep. In the mornings, after breakfast, there was half an hour to sing and meditate on a relevant passage from the Bible for that day before they left for the Casa Aberta.

'Before going to sleep the boys love to hear about my story of the streets of gold,' Marcia told me later. 'I tell them: when we open our hearts to Jesus we walk on streets of gold. When we believe, we walk on streets of gold. Not on streets made of tarmac, not on streets full of dust, full of litter, robbery and glue-sniffing. But streets made of gold, where there is purity, where the presence of Jesus is constant, where there is joy and everlasting love.'

*

Rone, Ronilson, Jairo, Josevaldo, Messias and Faisal were the first boys to be referred on to the farm from Casa Emmaus. Rone, twelve years old, was shy and sensitive. He had lived with his mother and sister in sub-human conditions in a favela called Minas Caixa west of the city centre. Their tiny one-room hut had no water or sewage system. A tin bucket placed outside the front door served as their lavatory, and human and dog faeces covered in flies were a permanent feature around the hut. Inside there was a single bed, a cupboard, an old stove and a table with a couple of chairs. Rone's father had left after his mother began to drink. Neighbours said that she sold anything she could in order to buy cachaca. Often Rone's nine-year-old sister was left on her own until two in the morning while their mother drank in bars. Rone had run away to the streets alone. 'My dream,' Rone said later, 'is that my mother stops drinking and that my father goes back to live with her and that the two live happily ever after.'

Ronilson, twelve years old, was sharp-witted and very persuasive. His mother had had five children from three different men. The youngest child had died from an untreated ear infection that had eventually passed to his heart. The family lived in a small house in a favela called Veneza. Their home had one bedroom which the mother had divided into two. She and her latest lover and children slept in one half, and her fifteen-year-old daughter with her twenty-three-year-old boyfriend slept in the other. Her daughter had lost her first baby. The lavatory was a hole in the ground behind the double bed and the kitchen was in the small corridor leading to the bedroom from the front door. Ronilson eventually ran away to the streets, where he'd stayed for three weeks before our street team took him to Casa Emmaus. It was essential to take the 'new street kids' off the streets as quickly as possible before they became part of a gang and got into bad habits.

Jairo, eleven years old, was very aggressive and difficult when he arrived in Casa Aberta. Small and skinny with black velvet skin, Jairo soon changed dramatically after he left the streets, and became affectionate and calm. His parents had separated and he and his older brother, Joilton, had gone to the streets. Although they lived in a favela their house had three bedrooms, a sitting room, bathroom and kitchen; plenty of room for a family with five children. His parents, however, had got back together again and wanted Jairo to return to live with them; his mother had become a Christian and his father had stopped going to the Macumba centre. In such a case as this we decided that Jairo needed six months of recuperation on the farm before returning to live with his family. Meanwhile, his parents needed therapy with Dr Silvia.

Messias was fourteen years old when he arrived at the farm. He had spent his life on the streets from the age of seven, after his father had died and his mother had gone to Sao Paulo. His two older brothers had taken him to the streets, he told me later. 'I lived on the streets for four years. During these four years I joined various gangs. At night there would often be *guerras* [street wars] between the gangs, but fortunately I was never knifed.' Messias went to prison three times. The street team eventually took him to Casa Emmaus.

Faisal lived on the streets for four years. He had left home because his mother was permanently drunk and took drugs. She had separated from Faisal's father, and her new boyfriend was a drug trafficker. 'My mother beat me a lot, and once she attacked me with a knife. She said I was responsible for her separation from my father. She doesn't like the fact that my name is the same as his.' On the streets Faisal ran with the worst gangs, Marcia, Vampirinho and Darley. He stole, sniffed glue and solvent and used marijuana. He went to prison; 'There they put me to sleep on a cold floor which was wet with urine. They made me do lots of very difficult exercises and if I made a mistake they beat and kicked me.' Faisal was fourteen years old, and slim with olive skin and brown eyes; it was easy to see that his grandfather was an Arab.

Josevaldo didn't know how old he was. He'd left his home in Bahia, north Brazil, three years earlier, after his parents had separated.

One thing we learned from the start was that if a boy didn't want to change, if he hadn't recognised that he needed to change, then he couldn't be helped. If he didn't want help there was absolutely nothing we could do to persuade him he did. And what would inevitably happen in these cases was that they would end up exhausting the team and influencing the other boys on the farm with bad habits and bad attitudes. The overall work would be affected dramatically.

In October of the previous year Rodrigo, aged fourteen, came to the farm after six years of living on the streets. In the month he was with us he managed to cause a problem every single day. In fact, the only person he liked and with whom he was himself was Lucas, my son, who was one year old at the time!

He didn't want to study or work on the farm, he didn't want responsibilities, he didn't want to comply with the rules, he only wanted to play. He threatened us every day that he'd leave and go back to the streets just to get what he wanted. Everything came to a head one morning, when we were woken up in the early hours with the news that Rodrigo was halfway up the drive to the main road taking six of the other children with him. When we managed to call them all back, every single one of them was in a state about something and only Rodrigo was calm. He'd managed to wind each one of them up with a reason to go back to the street.

'My brother's still on the streets and Rodrigo told me he's in danger,' shouted Juarez angrily.

'Tio Mauro gave me another discipline yesterday, he's always giving me disciplines,' exaggerated Washington.

'It's a horrible place here,' lied Wallace.

Eventually they all calmed down and apologised. The only person who said nothing was Rodrigo.

The following Sunday Rodrigo ran back to the streets during the morning service at the Lagoinha church in Belo Horizonte.

The farm is not a prison; it is a beautiful place that God has given them, a place where they can become children again, where their lives are restored. However, none of them are forced to stay. The choice to stay and change is theirs.

A month after the first group of boys had arrived on the farm from Casa Emmaus, Douglas, Wallace, Igor and Davidson also arrived. They had only spent a week in the shelter and their preparation time was not sufficient, as we were soon to find out. Wallace was a leader of a gang in the city and had been on the streets for more than six years, as had Douglas. Igor and Davidson had lived on the streets for only a few months, and their families wanted them back. Both of these families were in the middle of therapy and it was decided that Igor and Davidson needed a three-month period of recuperation on the farm. However, after one week Wallace went back to lead his gang, and Douglas ran back to the streets taking Igor with him, promptly dumping him in Belo and joining a gang on their way to Victoria. And Davidson left taking Josevaldo with him. Josevaldo and Igor both quickly realised that what they'd done was a mistake and wanted to come back to the farm immediately. In the case of Igor we decided it best he return to live with his mother, and Josevaldo went back to Casa Emmaus. We could not always accept boys back on the farm after they'd run off, otherwise the other boys would lose the value they had for the farm and running away on a bad day would become a habit rather than something taken seriously. We decided the time had come to take Josevaldo back to Bahia to trace his long-lost family. Anderson returned triumphantly from the trip a week later, having found his mother's house and delighted brothers, sisters and aunts, all of whom had apparently welcomed their long-lost Josevaldo with open arms.

Not only were the lives of these boys changing on the farm, but so was the farm itself! In two years it had been transformed. Joao had managed to get the local council to provide large bulldozers which had cut through the land, providing more space to build. One thousand five hundred metres of new roads were opened up, and down the hill by the stream machines cut through the thickness of the undergrowth and woodland providing an area large enough to dig three large lakes for fish farming, a swimming pool, a sand volleyball court, a vegetable garden and fields to plant corn and *mandioca* (a root plant). Two telephone lines were installed, linking up with lines one and a half kilometres from Ravena. All the team and the boys helped in the construction of all these innovations, and it proved an invaluable experience as once again we saw God providing the finances to buy the materials. The sense of unity grew strong as together we started and finished each project.

Our team had also grown on the farm. Ricardo had left to go to Russia as a missionary with his new English wife, so Mauro had taken over the co-ordination of the work on the farm, and Ilce, together with Jessica from my church in London, the teaching and visiting of the families. Vanderley had joined us from the state of Espirito Santo, Janilde from the Baptist church in Belo Horizonte, and Will and Flora, also from Holy Trinity Brompton, spent several months with us. Flora, who is a nurse, was able to apply her training daily to the medical needs of the children, most of whom arrive with worms, bad infections and viruses. Ingrid, a music teacher from Germany who had first read about our work in Ireland where she was working with Youth With A Mission, had also joined to teach the children singing and music. It was encouraging to see how talented many of the children were musically, and learning to play the recorder proved an important part in their restoration. Diana, an art and design graduate from England, came to teach them art. Her creative flair rubbed off on the boys, and it was great to see them making mobiles with colourful parrots from pieces of cardboard, decorations from pine-cones and bits of dried flowers, pop-up pictures brightly painted, large wall collages and cards. Even the most untalented enjoyed being artistic as a whole new area of creativity was opened up in their lives.

In April of that year Joao had been invited to speak about our work in the city Presbyterian church one Saturday night. It was a regular youth meeting which had started years earlier in order to reach the punks, hippies and drug addicts; over two thousand people came. There was always a guest band and a guest speaker. Joao decided to take Welbert and Carlos with him to give their testimonies; after all, they could tell their stories better than he could. The place was packed full with young people, and after the band had stopped playing Carlos stood up and, taking the microphone, gave his testimony. People wept as he told them how Jesus had taken him from the streets and given him a new life. How Satan had been destroying his life with drugs, stealing, lies, fights; he'd even lost his right eye. But that now he had a life worth living: he was studying and working, but above all he now knew the tremendous love that Jesus had for him. Carlos was shy at the best of times and always found it hard to look a person in the face when talking to them. However, when he spoke in front of thousands that night there was absolutely no sign of timidity.

Welbert then stood up to speak and as soon as he took the microphone there was a hush and the whole place fell silent once again. Completely overcome by the presence of God, Welbert could say nothing for at least thirty seconds. Eventually, looking up, he said, 'I feel Jesus is here and He wants to bless each of you this night.'

Suddenly people started praying on one side of the auditorium. Then all at once Welbert began to pray in tongues over the microphone and God started to minister to everyone there. After fifteen minutes Joao took the microphone from Welbert and said, 'I believe there are people here tonight who want to ask Jesus into their lives for the first time. And there are others who want to recommit their lives to Jesus.'

That night over three hundred people went forward to pray.

11

The Good Samaritan

'Pastor Marcio has agreed to sell the farm to us,' announced Joao, overjoyed, during a team meeting. 'However, our purpose is to restore children's lives, rescuing them from the streets and placing them back in their families,' he continued, 'and I don't want to take everyone's attention from this in order to raise money to buy the farm. We are tending around sixty-five children between the three homes each week and I don't want this to change. Our objective here is not to buy property or to build buildings. Sure, we need these things, but it's not to become our priority.'

June 1995 saw the start of what would be a very cold winter in Belo Horizonte. The temperature started dropping drastically from 23°C during the day to as low as 3°C at night. We became concerned about the families of the children we were helping in the favelas, many of whom had no blankets, beds, mattresses, cookers, warm clothing or sufficient food. We called an emergency team meeting at the farm, and with everyone from all the three houses there were about thirty of us in total.

'Rather than worrying about our need,' explained Joao, 'let's supply the needs of others and leave God to raise the money for the farm. God has told me that the winter will get even colder here over the next two months. Let's start a new campaign involving the local churches. We can speak over the next few Sundays in some churches, together with the boys, and invite the congregation to participate by giving clothes, food, medicines, furniture, kitchen and laundry equipment and blankets to the children's needy families. We will need to find a vehicle that can pick up these donations from people's houses and a place in the city where we can store the donations before distributing them to the families in the favelas. Let's pray, and then I will go and speak to Pastor Marcio for his advice and confirmation.'

Pastor Marcio said immediately that the campaign had come from God. What's more, he had a friend who had a warehouse close to the Lagoinha church. His name was Claudio, a member of the Full Gospel Businessmen's Fellowship and a former owner of a large furniture business. The warehouse, 2000 square metres in size with two floors, had been closed for several years but he was planning to give it to his nineteen-year-old son who had just finished at journalism school. Joao arranged a meeting at the Lagoinha church with Claudio and Pastor Jonas, who was the second pastor under Marcio. Claudio quickly explained that three other people had approached him that week offering a lot of money to rent the warehouse. Joao shared about our need for a place in the city to collect the donations for the families, but emphasised that we had no means to rent it. Claudio agreed to think and pray about it for a week.

A week later the phone rang at the farm. Joao answered it.

'Look,' said Claudio, 'God has always put on my heart the desire to use the warehouse for His work and I recognise that this campaign will help many people. I'm not going to rent it out to these other businessmen, nor is my son going to start up the furniture business again. As a matter of fact, he was offered a great job as a journalist just last week. You can use it over the next three months, free of charge.'

The following month we spoke in four churches: the Lagoinha, the Central Baptist, the Communidade and the Baptist church in Bairro Preto. Eleven of the boys sang songs Ingrid had taught them, including some in English such as, 'Heaven is a wonderful place' and 'Jesus, I love You deep down in my heart'. Anderson and Jose Carlos played so beautifully on the recorder that a shiver went up my spine every time they performed, and it was difficult to find a dry eye in the congregation. Wender and Jose Roberto gave their testimonies and shared first-hand the reality of life in the favelas and the real needs of their families. Oades had helped design a leaflet about the campaign which was called *Bom Samaritano* (the Good Samaritan). This was, after all, the motivation of the campaign: to give to your neighbour, to share what you had with someone who did not. The leaflets were handed out in their hundreds and the t-shirts we'd made up sold like hot cakes.

There was one other problem. We didn't have enough people to visit all the families and distribute the donations. This was, however, to be solved quicker than we thought. On the very day Joao had gone to the Lagoinha church to have his meeting with Claudio he had met Willar in the canteen on his way out. Willar turned out to be the leader of a large evangelistic youth group of more than two hundred people in the church, called IDE (GO!). When Joao had finished sharing about the campaign Willar declared, 'Joao, this is my project. For three months this very campaign has been sitting in my drawer. I just didn't know how to start it. If everything works out with the warehouse, and Pastor Marcio agrees, then my group are with you 100 per cent.'

'Pastor Marcio agreed. And Joao and I went to speak to the group one Thursday night. At the end of the meeting fifty people put their hands up volunteering to help, and someone offered their small pick-up truck.

'It's great that there are so many of you who want to help,' I said with a big smile, 'but it's a good idea to pray about it first, because it's easy to go by your emotions on the spur of the moment.'

They went away to pray, and the fifty went down to twenty. Ademir, one of the co-founders of the group, took over the leadership of co-ordinating the visits to the families and distributing the donations. Their first challenge, however, was cleaning the warehouse which was thick with dust.

Ilce, at the farm, received the telephone calls from the people giving the various donations and passed them on to Ademir, who in turn had them picked up and taken to the warehouse. Then, together with either Ilce or Ingrid at the farm or Kevin and his team in Casa Emmaus and the Casa Aberta they visited the respective families of the children. We started to receive washing machines, cookers, blankets, sofas, mattresses, beds, cupboards, tables, chairs, clothes, shoes, toys and ninety Cesta Basicas.

Derson's mother received one of the washing machines. She had formerly had to spend all her free time washing the clothes for her seven children, and lines of washing could be seen daily hanging around her one-room house. Fortunately there was running water and electricity and before long the machine was washing the clothes for her!

The need for a place where the families of our boys could have regular Bible teaching, care and assistance became more and more crucial. There were simply too many families for us to visit weekly. Then one day Ademir suggested to us, 'The Lagoinha church has 121 *grupos de crescimento* [home groups] around the city. They meet up once a week to study the Bible, pray and generally help one another. I myself am a leader of one of these groups and meet up regularly with the other leaders to discuss and pray about various issues. Most of these families have one of the groups nearby and I could speak to the leader of each respective group, take them to meet the family concerned and they in turn can take over the pastoral care for us on a weekly basis.'

This was the plan God had spoken to me about a year earlier.

Joao Leite, who had been Brazil's goalkeeper in the late eighties and who was co-founder and leader of Athletes for Christ in his country, was elected *Deputado Estadual* (State Deputy) for Minas Gerais in 1995. He was not only a member of the Central Baptist church, where we operate our Casa Aberta, but was personally concerned about helping the street children, something he did wholeheartedly. A good friend of his, Jose Carlos, happened to be the general director of Bon Marche, the third largest supermarket chain in Brazil. Jose Carlos also had a big heart for the street children and wanted to give an opportunity for them to have a profession. He didn't want publicity for doing so, he was simply worried about the social situation in the country and wanted to give his assistance. He opened up job opportunities for ten of our teenagers of fourteen years and over.

Eight of our teenagers from the farm were restored and ready to work; Marcos, Faisal and Edson were employed in the meat section of the supermarket, Messias and Welbert in the bakery section, Januario and Mauro in the vegetable section and Oades in the marketing and decoration department. The salary was good for six hours' work per day, including breakfast, lunch and dinner. Transport was also paid for, and all medical and dentistry assistance was free. After one year of working at the supermarket the boys could study at private school, all paid for, and after five years they could receive a grant to go to university if they so wanted.

I will never forget the first time I saw them in their uniforms working in the supermarket: Marcos all friendly smiles as he chatted away to his customers while weighing out some sausages, Januario re-stocking the vegetable section with fresh lettuces and green peppers, Messias and Welbert standing behind a spectacular display of fresh bread rolls, croissants, french bread and sweet cakes, many of which they'd made themselves. I could feel tears burning the back of my eyes; only a few months earlier they'd been on the streets forgotten and lost, I thought to myself, and now here they were cared for and full of hope in the promise of a bright future.

They were studying after work at schools close by the

supermarket. All of the boys had lost five to six years of school but were studying two years in one. Every Monday and Wednesday, between work, dinner and school, Ademir was spending time with them studying the Bible, discussing problems they had in relationships among themselves or with work colleagues and other important issues for the boys, like dating! On Tuesdays they had extra tuition time with a teacher we contracted, and on Thursdays a psychologist spent time with them, generally helping them to integrate into society and to solve any remaining relationship problems with their families.

Most of these boys were unable to return to their families for a variety of reasons. At the same time they were now at the age when they needed more privacy and personal freedom, where they could develop initiative, learn to make decisions, in other words be more independent. We started to pray and look for an apartment to rent near to the supermarket where six teenagers could live with two workers; it would be a Casa Republica.

After their first month working for Bon Marche Joao and I had a chat with them all, including Jose Roberto and Carlos who were also working.

'So,' said Joao with a smile, 'tell us, one by one, who spent their salary on what this month.' They all looked at one another sideways. 'Jose Roberto, you start.'

One by one they confessed that all their money had gone on a pair of trainers, jeans, a t-shirt; some had bought small video games, Coca-Cola, snacks, ice-cream. Only Januario and Messias had thought about others, buying trainers for Jardel and Rone who lived on the farm. No one had bought food for their families.

191

'All of you have a relationship with Jesus and I want to encourage you to start to sow every month,' said Joao. 'This is the way this ministry started. It is the way the kingdom of God works; give, give, give. When you sow God gives you much more. You only have to look at the world of nature around you to understand that God likes to multiply. It's time you separated 10 per cent of your salary to give to the church you are attending. And it is important that you open a savings account to save for the future. Maybe it can go towards a training for a profession, or a present for someone you want to help, or a bicycle. It's time to give yourselves limits, to think about others and to save.'

On July 27th our second son, Daniel John, was born. Lucas took to him immediately, calling him *nenem* which means baby in Portuguese. On my arrival back home on the farm from the hospital, I was to find a string of brightly coloured pictures festooned around the front of the house, all done by the boys to welcome Daniel into the family. One by one all the boys came to have a look at him in the pram. Like Lucas, he has brought everyone tremendous joy.

It never failed to impress me how God alerted us to pray when all was not right among our team or the boys, or if He was going to release something to the ministry, be it money, a new house or a new project. As leaders we would always be the first to know. I might add that this experience happens rarely rather than often. One Thursday morning in the middle of August, I woke up with a heavy oppressive feeling and at the same time the peace I

so enjoyed had gone; in its place I felt only restlessness.
Joao had had nightmares of a demonically possessed man
trying to deceive and harm him and Lucas had uncharac-
teristically woken up screaming for no reason at all at
various intervals during the night. My household was
not peaceful. We came together to ask God what was
going on. Immediately three thoughts came into my
mind: money, church and Casa Republica. We had received a disjointed fax a few days earlier from Caroline
Taylor in England saying, 'I received a phone call from
someone asking for your bank details in America. Get
praying, because if I heard right you could possibly receive
a large offering towards the farm.' Also, the previous
night we had just started a church on the farm to reach
the three thousand inhabitants of Ravena, our next-door
neighbours.

'Joao,' I said, 'I believe God needs us to pray for three
things urgently. The church we have started which will
eventually be planted in Ravena itself; the release of the
money towards the farm; and it appears the time has
arrived to open a Casa Republica for the teenagers in the
city.'

Immediately we called for a meeting with everyone on
the farm. This also included our two visiting teams from
Tear Fund and the home church and university of Mark
Hester, one of our first short-term overseas helpers.
Together it made for quite a gathering and as we started
to sing and exalt the Lord the presence of the Holy Spirit
came and I once again felt a deep warmth throughout my
whole being. Interestingly, instead of praying for these
three things we were led to pray for one another. Unity of
course was what God wanted first. Then after two hours

three of us simply prayed out in faith, in the name of Jesus, that these three things would happen.

Two days later Jim Wimberley, the co-ordinator of the Happy Child Mission charity in the USA, telephoned.

'It's a miracle!' cried Jim on the other end of the line. 'Someone from Singapore has deposited $US50,000 into the Happy Child account today. The money is specifically to be used for the purchase of the farm!'

We were beside ourselves, jumping up and down like little children.

'Did they give their name? We don't know anyone living in Singapore,' asked Joao, smiling from ear to ear.

'No, they didn't. This is a miracle,' continued Jim, laughing with joy.

We had done the possible, helping the families through the Good Samaritan campaign, and God had done the impossible, raising $US50,000 towards the farm.

A few weeks later, we asked Pastor Renatto, a personal friend and pastor of a church in Belo Horizonte, the Igreja Batista de Ouro Preto, if he would like to pastor the church we'd started and make it a plant of his own church. He accepted.

Once the church has grown in numbers and a location is obtained we plan to open a crèche during the week. Ravena is full of young single mothers who cannot work because there is nowhere to leave their children.

Around the same time, while driving around the neighbourhood close to Bon Marche, Joao suddenly saw a 'For Rent' sign over a two-storey house three blocks from the supermarket. The first thing the owner, an elderly lady, said to Joao as she showed him in through the front door of the first floor apartment was, 'I plan to rent this apartment to a couple with young children. Teenagers are absolutely out of the question.'

Joao laughed as he said, 'So in that case I'm going to rent it for our Casa Republica with six teenagers and two workers!'

Apparently she looked at him aghast, and burst out laughing, sure that he'd made a joke.

The apartment was bright and spacious with two large bedrooms, a bathroom, sitting room, large dining area, kitchen and a small area for a washing machine. The whole place had been freshly painted inside and out, and brown wooden shutters sat either side of the large windows. A balcony with ornate wooden panelling went around the front of the apartment.

It turned out that the elderly lady attended the Presbyterian church and Joao went on to explain about our work. By the end of the conversation she had completely changed her mind.

'Listen, you are my preference above the other two people who have already visited this apartment. What's more, I'll reduce the rent from $US600 per month to $US520. Go and speak to my lawyer and tell him I've changed my mind about teenagers living here.'

The lawyer didn't believe Joao's story, and telephoned the old lady for confirmation. One week later we had rented the apartment.

On August 27th Pastor Marcio baptised nine of the boys in our swimming pool at the farm. It was an occasion for celebration, and we invited more than one hundred and seventy friends and partners involved with our work to witness the event and for a buffet and barbecue lunch. The boys had taken a discipleship course in preparation for the baptism. And it was a victorious day for our Lord as Oades, Carlos, Welbert, Januario, Edson, Marcos, Jose Roberto, Messias and Eduardo entered the water, each one of their faces expressing the emotion and importance of this moment in their lives.

Eduardo, now fourteen years old, had only recently come back to the farm. After running away from the family foster home, he had soon returned to the streets and become a leader of a gang, stealing, fighting and taking drugs once again. Occasionally he would telephone Joao and me for a chat from a pay-phone on the streets and we would tell him that he had to make the decision to change, we couldn't make it for him. All this time, however, we were praying for him, and during one prayer time I saw a picture in my mind of Jesus weeping over the life of Eduardo. After two months, during one of the coldest winters, Eduardo went to the Casa Emmaus. On the day he arrived in the shelter they had problems with the water system and all the boys had to come to stay on the farm for the weekend. Eduardo never went back.

'My first week on the farm was a battle,' Eduardo told me later.

'I felt really tired and heavy all the time and only had bad thoughts of fighting and running away back to the streets. Then Joao prayed for some of us before we were baptised and when it was my turn I wept and wept. It was great to be able to confess the things I'd done wrong and to be forgiven. I felt so light afterwards.'

After he was baptised, Eduardo told me, 'When I came out of the water it was as though the old Eduardo stayed behind in the water and a new me came out. For a week afterwards I felt so light and free, when I walked it was as though my feet didn't touch the ground. I am going to be a missionary for God.'

Two weeks later, without any warning or explanation, Carlos dropped out of school, threw up his job in the timber company run by a friend of ours, and left the farm. He went to live with his older brother in an old chicken-run by his aunt's house in a favela, and took up selling pens door-to-door. In our great sadness, we remembered the words of Suzanne, the leader of JEAME (an organis-ation working with street children for over thirteen years in Sao Paulo), when she taught at a seminar here a year ago: 'If these children decide to rebel and return to their old ways, there is nothing you can physically do about it. It is only when they hit rock bottom that they may come back, only this time they are more humble than before, and they seek the will of God for their lives with all their might.' So we continued to pray for Carlos, encouraged by the words of his testimony (see chapter 12) '. . . we get to know Jesus and we never leave Him again'.

Six weeks later, Carlos came back to the farm, thinner and with his head bent low.

'I'm sorry I left, it was a big mistake,' he said, not able to make eye contact. 'Please give me another chance.'

In August 1995, we had the first meeting to pray and discuss the vision for Africa which God long ago put on our hearts: we plan to begin a Crianca Feliz ministry in Mozambique. Mark Hester, who shares our vision and has been praying for the country for some time, was with us, on his third working visit to the farm, and we invited him to be leader of our team. Eight of us attended the meeting, including Welbert; and it was exciting to hear how God had already called each one of us to help rescue the orphans in this poverty-stricken land. Mozambique, whose language is also Portuguese, is the poorest country in the world economically, and millions of children are in dire straits. After years of brutal civil war, during which more than one million people died and almost six million became refugees, there is little work available. Today it is the women, often pregnant or with babies strapped to their backs, who do the heavy labour, working in the fields. We envisage a farm with an emphasis on self-sufficiency, with the same structure and principles as here in Belo Horizonte, but on a larger scale.

In September 1995, Pastor Marcio called Joao for a meeting in his office. There he suggested that we buy another farm for the church in exchange for the farm in Ravena, which he eventually estimated to be worth around $US220,000.

For three solid months Joao looked at dozens of farms but could not find anything suitable for the church. Finally, just before Christmas, he found a beautiful farm in a peaceful setting one hour's drive from Belo Horizonte. It was smaller than our farm in Ravena but had a large elegant house, lakes and dormitories for up to fifty people. Underneath the main house there was an exquisite chapel for prayer. They said they'd sell it to us for $US84,000.

In February 1996 we received another donation from the same family in Singapore for $US50,000 with a note saying, 'I hope and pray that this will enable Criana Feliz to secure the farm.' It was yet again time to thank God for His incredible faithfulness.

With this second donation we were able to buy the smaller farm for the church which in turn secured the farm in Ravena for our work with the street children. We agreed to pay a further $US136,000 in ten instalments which the church will use to build seven classrooms needed to enlarge their popular school. As Pastor Marcio said, 'I believe that God wants to bless both sides with this transaction, the church and Crianca Feliz.'

We were half way there.

12

'Let the Children Speak . . .'

This chapter gives some of the children and teenagers who have passed through the programme at Crianca Feliz the opportunity to give their own testimonies. After all, although I may have given a brief outline of their histories in an earlier chapter, they can each tell their story far better than me.

Welbert Eustaquio de Oliveira. Born: 25.3.79

In my home there was no unity, only fighting. One time when I was about five years old my mother asked me to buy some bread. She was pregnant at the time. She told me to get money from my father, who was in the local bar. When I arrived at the bar they told me that he was in the house next door. There I found my father in bed with another woman. It was terrible – I remember it vividly to this day. I ran to my mother to tell her and she picked up a hot frying-pan full of eggs and went into this woman's house and hit them both with it. I was watching. My father started hitting my mother, and she ran out of the house shouting and screaming. From that day I had a lot of anger against my father.

When I was ten years old I started to know the streets.

Begging for money, travelling on the back bumper of buses, robbing money from the smaller kids on the streets. I never studied at school; I started a few times but never stayed for very long. Soon I had made friends with other street kids. Whenever I went home there was no love, no affection, no peace and so I decided to stay on the streets where at least I had friends.

But I had no happiness, only a deep hate for life. I started to take drugs and to rob on a regular basis with gangs. Every gang adopts the name of its leader, be it a male or a female. We never robbed for the leader; in fact he was the one who had to rob the most in order to gain respect from the others. The leader was always the most violent as well, terrifying everyone into obedience.

We always went out to steal in twos. One kept watch and gave the signal and the other stole. Then the two divided the money or goods between them. We had to steal to survive. The girls in the gangs always ran the greatest risk living on the street; rape, beatings. If they were caught with another guy other than their boyfriend they were burnt and tortured. Girls of eight and ten years old had sex with the boys their age and younger. Girls of fourteen to eighteen years old were prostitutes. Sometimes when the police arrested us they would take our stolen goods for keeps and let us go free.

On the streets I felt as though someone was trying to destroy me and at the same time that someone else was trying to protect me. I ran into various risks on the streets. My life was threatened often and the police were after me. A gang leader called Cabecao [Large-head], he was only thirteen years old, caught me once and demanded that I give him cigarettes and drugs only I didn't have any on me at the time. So he took a lit cigarette and started to burn my chest and arms with it.

At this point I had already started going to the Casa Aberta so I had a small understanding of God. But I would lie to the workers there, telling them that I had stopped taking drugs, and then as soon as I left the Centre I would sniff glue.

Then one day the police arrested me. I had stolen a lot of chocolate from a shop. The woman from the shop had said to me, 'Don't steal, son, leave the chocolate alone.' She was probably a Christian. But I didn't listen and as I ran out of the shop I went straight into some policemen and all the chocolate that I'd stuffed up my shirt fell to the ground. They grabbed me and started to beat me with their boots. I fought back and managed to get away. I was very smart and quick on the streets and they lost me.

I lived on the streets for three years and looking back I can see that I was protected from death. I believe it was because people were praying for me. Really the only things that affected my life badly were the drugs.

At the Casa Aberta I started to learn about obedience, manners, how to serve others, how to be more humble. I had a lot of pride and jealousy. I always had to be the first.

When I came to the farm over a year ago, it was like I had to start my life all over again. I was given responsibilities on the land and the challenge was to finish what I had started. This was difficult at the beginning because I didn't like people telling me what to do.

I asked Jesus into my life four times. The first time was just to show the people around me. The second time I still really didn't know what I was doing. The third time I had a lot more understanding of who Jesus was, and I was in the church and I went to the front and asked one more time. After this I had a desire to read the Bible more. The fourth and final time was on the farm, and I wept and wept afterwards.

I'd started to see that Jesus was real and how much He loved me. For example, if it wasn't for the love of Jesus Christ, there is no way all these street boys would stay on this farm. Also, another example, Sarah, Joao and the other workers – there is no way they would leave their families, homes and jobs if Jesus wasn't real.

Then God put Ricardo (the co-ordinator on the farm) in my life and he was like a pastor for me, always there to guide me back on to the right path when I was really struggling. I had so much anger still and would often beat up the other boys. However, slowly, slowly God started to take this anger from me.

It was like I was a piece of ice and the workers were like fire around me and I was melting. The more I sought God through prayer and worship the more my life changed. Today I don't have any more anger, only peace and a deep sense of being loved.

One time in church last year Jose Roberto and I had such a strong desire to speak in tongues. Only I was very selfish and I only wanted this for myself, I wanted to be first again. This attitude was a barrier for me at first, because the Holy Spirit is not just for one person but for everyone. Then the pastor came and prayed for me and Jose, and suddenly I just felt as though I was being filled up and filled up with joy and I started to laugh and laugh. Jose started to speak in tongues. I couldn't open my eyes at first because I just wanted to praise God.

At Christmastime a team from Sarah's church, Holy

Trinity Brompton in London, came for a month. They prayed for me and once again I felt this incredible joy flooding my body. Then I had a vision and I saw an arm extending out towards me, and I cried out loud, 'I want to go, I want to go!' And then I heard a voice saying to me, 'No, it's not the right time yet, but I will use you in My work in the future.' It was Jesus.

Today I am working for the large supermarket Bon Marche and I am able to help my mother buy food and pay some bills. At night I am studying in the city. I only want to do the will of God for my life, I know He will give me many more opportunities. This is just the beginning.

Welbert was baptised on August 27th 1995. He is now working for Bon Marche supermarket in the city and living with his mother and brothers.

Carlos Rock da Silva. Born: 17.12.79

My name is Carlos Rock. I am fifteen years old. I have been on the farm for nearly a year. I was born in Taquaracu in Minas Gerais. I would like to tell you a bit about my life, how I was before I became a Christian.

My life was very sad. I lived on the streets, robbing and sniffing glue. I was very bad to others around me. I was on and off the streets for over a year and I used to stay alone, I didn't join a gang. It was very lonely. Sometimes Satan offered you things that you thought were good and it wasn't so good after all. Not as good as a life with Jesus. But sometimes I felt sad because I was far away from my mother, and other times I felt sorry for the very people that I'd harmed.

I started to wash cars near the bus station, Plaza Estacao, to help my mother. There was a gang, a very dangerous gang, called Marcia and they used to watch me for when I had money. One night they circled me. When I turned around a fat boy, a really big guy, hit me in the eye with one of those long fluorescent light bulbs. A school bus was passing and the driver stopped to help me. He alerted the police who were near by and they took me to the hospital. They caught the boy and he went to the jail. I stayed in the hospital for ten days; my eye was hurting so much, it felt like it was going to fall out. They operated but couldn't save my sight and today I am blind in my right eye.

Soon after this, last year I met a guy on the streets who I'd known for a long time called Kleber [one of the teenagers who was with the Mission]. We were near the bus station in Belo Horizonte, and he took me to a church [in fact the Casa Aberta] where they help street children, giving them food, and they speak about the word of God. It was there that I started to seek God but I still hadn't converted, I still smoked and did bad things. Then I started to pray and after a while I went to a farm in Ravena. A wonderful house, a house of God. And here we pray and get to know Jesus and we never leave Him again.

When I was prayed for to receive the Holy Spirit, for the first time in my life I saw a vision, God showed me that angels were working on my heart. It was like seeing a spiritual operation. After this I really started to pray.

Juarez Santos Barbosa. Born: 2.11.84

My name is Juarez, folks, I am ten years old and I would like to share with you how I suffered in my life. I used to live on the streets with my brother Washington. I left home because my mother drank a lot and beat me. Once she broke a sound system over the head of my father; he left her. She died a few years ago of alcohol.

On the streets I fought with the other kids and I sniffed glue once but I knew that it wasn't good for me so I stopped and to this day I have never sniffed drugs again. We slept in a tree, by putting a plank of wood between branches. Nobody knew about it. The worst thing was at night, it was so cold and I couldn't sleep properly.

One day we met a woman called Gemima [the cook in the Casa Aberta] and she gave us a blanket. Then she took us to the Casa Aberta. After a few weeks we came to the farm. Here I am very happy and I am full of peace. I have a new life, a good life, and I know that God is doing something wonderful in my life.

Anderson Pereira dos Santos. Born: 22.7.82

My name is Anderson and I am twelve years old. I was born in Salto da Divisa, Bahia. When I was small my mother moved to Belo Horizonte. I don't know my father. She married and had another four children. My stepfather and his family didn't like me because I wasn't his son. I used to go to the streets to wash cars and earn some money and I'd return home at 5.00 p.m. and he would beat me. His family tried to send me away on various occasions. But I did things wrong too, I sometimes stole money from my mother.

Once he tried to kill my mother with a knife. He had another woman, and my mother sent him out of the house. One day he came back and attacked her with a knife.

I ran away to the streets, and stayed with Julio and others for almost a year. We would beg for food and someone gave us a blanket. We would hide it in a pothole during the day. On the streets I sniffed glue and robbed on various occasions. I stole milk from shop doorways early in the mornings and bread to eat. But I felt very guilty about stealing. I walked around with bare feet and wore an extra-large t-shirt which helped keep me warm at night. Sometimes I would really miss my mother and one night at the beginning I cried.

Then one day we went to the Casa Aberta. I stayed there for a month before I came to the farm.

Jesus took me out of the streets, He rescued me from all this and He gave me a good life. Here on the farm each one of us is an example of this. Here I have learned to love others and to obey the workers, because God loves me. Jesus has healed me. When I arrived I had a lot of anger against my stepfather, but it has all gone and I have forgiven him. But sometimes I still tell lies.

When I was prayed for last year I saw a picture of clouds and Jesus was there waiting for me. I felt really emotional and started to cry. He told me that He had forgiven me. I will never forget this moment, it is deep in my heart.

I would like to be a professional footballer.

Julio Cesar Martins Basilio. Born: 3.3.84

I am eleven years old. My brothers beat me up a lot. They'd wait for my mother to go to work and then they'd beat me up, often with pieces of wood. My house was really dirty. We would go to a place near by where there was lots of water to wash our clothes and to take showers.

I would run away from home every day. But on the streets it was even worse. At night it was cold and sometimes it would start to rain, I couldn't sleep until the early hours of the morning. I was filthy too and smelt bad. Twice I was nearly raped. The first time I was playing with a video game and I needed more tokens. The man in the shop told me to follow him up the stairs to the second floor. So I followed him and when we got to the top he turned around and grabbed me and tried to rape me, but I managed to get away. The second time it was raining and very cold and a man stopped me in the streets and said I could sleep in his house. When we arrived he tried to rape me, but he couldn't. I felt terrible, really sad.

One day the police caught me, beat me up and took me to the Cidade do Menor (a government home for street children). I stayed a long time there. Then I ran away and went back to the streets. We would steal clothes and shoes from balconies and windows. Once I tried to steal a bicycle but I didn't manage it. We were always on the run from the police.

One day someone from the Conselho Tutelar took me to the Casa Aberta. But I didn't go there every day. Eventually they sent me to the farm.

To begin with I cried a lot, because I was still very sad. Then one day I asked Jesus to come into my life, and today I am happy.

When I grow up I want to be the mayor of Belo Horizonte. Then I will help the poor, tell them about Jesus, help people get work. I am praying for my family [he has eleven brothers and sisters] that they too will know Jesus. I want to help my brothers.

*

His mother died suddenly in August 1995, the day after she'd paid a long-awaited visit to Julio on the farm. He eventually went to live with his father, who had become a Christian. Julio would pray more for his family than anyone!

Anderson Euzebio de Morais. Born: 22.1.85

My name is Derson. I am ten years old. At home I suffered a lot, my mother and my older brothers beat me and I would always leave. But I did things wrong too, once I fought with my younger brother and he hurt himself against the wall. My mother would drink. I didn't like her to drink. I would swear all the time, it was terrible. I didn't know my father, he died. My house has only one room, it is very small, but we had water. One day I ran away from home alone. I met three street boys and I was very scared so I started to run. I hid alone and started to sleep. But it started to rain and I felt really cold, then a lady gave me a blanket and I slept. The next day I went to the park, but some kids stole my money. I suffered so much. One day a car hit me in my back, it really hurt.

On the streets I stayed with Wender and two others, we would sleep near the main square in the city. At nights it was very difficult to sleep because of the cold.

Then some people took me to the Casa Aberta where I heard that Jesus loved me. Now I am praying for my mother and my brothers.

On the farm at Christmas some people prayed for me and I was filled with the Holy Spirit. I saw a picture of heaven with Jesus and His disciples, they were all white and looked like angels. Heaven is very beautiful.

Today I am full of happiness because Jesus changed my life. When I am older I want to be a doctor to help people who are dying and suffering.'

Jose Roberto Resende Silva (Ze). Born: 14.7.81

I was born in Rocas Novas in Minas Gerais and I am fourteen years old. I don't remember my father because he died of alcoholic poisoning when I was a baby. Apparently he was a big man, and an excellent musician. He played the violin. People always think I'm sixteen because I'm also very tall. And I have inherited my father's musical gifts, today I play the recorder and I want to learn to play the violin too. My parents had a girl and another boy before me but my brother died of heart problems.

After my father died my mother left my elder sister with my granny and brought me to Belo Horizonte. She found another man and had a baby. Then one day our small house burnt down with everything in it, so my mother didn't have the conditions to take care of the baby and she gave him to someone else. When I was six years old my mother put me into the Cidade do Menor. I was very unhappy there because the older boys always beat me up. The problem was that whenever they did anything wrong I used to tell the staff, and of course they didn't like this. One night they beat me up really badly, so I picked up two blankets and ran away into the fields and hid for two days and two nights alone. I cried a lot, and I felt very angry.

I was in the Cidade do Menor on and off for six years. I would spend some time on the street with Welbert and Oades and some time in the home. On the streets I stole from supermarkets. I didn't like stealing from people, I tried it once and stopped. We would beg for money and food. Drugs I received on the streets from other street boys.

My mother lives in one of the worst favelas in Belo Horizonte called Taquaril, I don't like it there. At one stage I didn't see her for over three years.

Then I started going to the Casa Aberta. After one month they sent me, Eduardo and Cristiano together to the farm. I will never forget when we arrived at the main gate of the farm, I nearly cried with happiness.

I liked it from the very beginning; working, studying. The only thing I didn't like was being disciplined!

Then I started to change. I discovered that Jesus can do marvellous things in our lives. I can remember the day that I asked Jesus into my life here on the farm, I suddenly felt much lighter. Also I always used to talk about death and I stopped immediately after this. All the anger left me.

Soon I had a strong desire to receive the Holy Spirit. I went to church with Welbert last year and the pastor prayed for us both. I couldn't keep my mouth shut and started speaking in tongues. Immediately I felt lighter, purer and full of joy. Now I know that the Jesus the people out there used to tell me about is real.

This year I started working in the city making gold and silver caps for teeth in a dentist's laboratory. One day I want to be a dentist.

I am studying at night school during the week. And I've decided that I want to get married when I'm nineteen years old!

After I asked Jesus into my life my relationship with my mother became much better. I never liked her before, and was ashamed of her. Now it's different. When I go and visit her she is so proud of me and wants to introduce me to all her neighbours. She tells them I'm a pastor!

One day I'm going to buy her a new house.

Ze was baptised in water on August 27th 1995. He is living in the Casa Republica in the city centre, the apartment for six teenagers now working and studying in the city.

Wender Rodrigues dos Santos. Born: 14.1.86.

I am nine years old. I didn't like to stay at home because my mother left us on our own often and sometimes she would beat me. I never knew my father, and I don't know what he looks like. My house has one room only. It is tiny and there is no water or toilet. There is only one bed where my mother slept with my sister and two baby brothers. I slept on the floor. And I used to have to fetch water.

When I was eight years old I took the bus into the city. There I met Derson and two other boys, we used to stay together. I stole three times, chocolate and small packets of popcorn. At night we put plastic on the ground because it was so cold.

One day we went to the Casa Aberta, I liked it there and went every day. In the mornings we would take a shower and have breakfast, then Roseanna [the teacher] taught us how to read and write. We would play sport in a place near to the Casa Aberta.

One day Selma [the co-ordinator] told me that there were two vacancies at the farm and that they were going to send me and Derson. I was very happy. On the farm I have my own bed, a blanket and regular meals. Here I learned to pray. God answers our prayers, He gave us a van! At the farm I work picking corn and other things, and I go to school.

When I am older I am going to be a pilot of aeroplanes.

Marcos Jose da Silva. Born: 2.5.83

My name is Marcos Silva and I am eleven years old. In my house I suffered because my father used to drink and he would hit me and beat me. One day he stuck a knife into my head because he thought I'd stolen some thing.

Eventually I took some of his money and ran away to the streets. I bought something to eat but soon the money ran out and I started to feel very hungry. I used to sleep on the streets near a place where a woman sold ice-cream. She used to give me ice-cream free. Then one day she took me to a house where I took a shower and received clean clothes. From there some people took me to the day-care centre where I played with the other kids.

Then I came to the farm. And here I asked Jesus into my life. Before, I was very angry, but God told me that I could forgive my father.

Today I am praying that I will go to live with my grandmother and my aunt.

Marcos is now living happily with his grandmother in the interior of Minas Gerais.

Januario de Almeida. Born: 6.6.79

My name is Januario and I am fifteen years old and I have been on the farm for over a year. I would like to share with you about my life, how I was before. When I lived in my house in Sabara I suffered very much. I did bad things too. I would stay on the streets begging for things, and I used to stand on the back bumper of moving buses. I would go to a Macumba centre which was near my house and drink wine that was offered to the demons. Also I used to go to the waterfall where they used to call the spirits and offer us things to drink. But I didn't know that it was dangerous at the time.

Then my mother locked us all in the house for nearly a year in the darkness. There were no windows, no light. The neighbours would pass food for us under the door. In the darkness Satan started to speak to me about stealing and killing. One day I went crazy and broke through the wall to get out.

Then Celso [from the local council] took me and my brother, Jardel, to the farm. Here I started to go to school in Ravena and have learned to read and write. Here I heard about Jesus, that He died for me.

One day some people prayed for me and I saw a picture. A demon was speaking to me, tormenting me and I was shaking with fear. Then Jesus arrived and spoke to us, saying that I didn't have to fear the bad things but that I should have faith in the word of God.

I am going to be a policeman.

Januario was baptised in water on August 27th 1995.

Washington Dos Santos Barbosa. Born: 29.5.82

My name is Washington and I am twelve years old. In my house I was always hungry because my mother didn't give us enough food. She would stay in the bar drinking. It was really terrible. She would always leave the house early. So in the end I decided to go to the streets and I took my brothers with me. But before this my younger brother Renatto would go to the streets alone, he is very young, six years old. Then I discovered that my mother was pregnant so I went back home. But I didn't stay for very long.

On the streets it was terrible too, I sniffed glue. One day my brother Joarez went to the Casa Aberta and they took him to the farm. I wondered where he had gone to so I too went to the Casa Aberta and asked where my brother was. They told me that if I continued going to the Centre I would also go to live on the farm. Then one night Anderson [the leader of street work] found me on the streets watching television through a shop window. And he took me to the farm. It was really great. Here is better because on the streets I had nothing.

I am full of happiness because my brother is here. God brought us to a better place. The streets only offer bad things.

When I am older I want to be a preacher for God.

Oades Farley Oliveira. Born: 4.8.80

I haven't heard from my mother for over six years and I don't know my father. When I was born my mother gave me to the couple who were running the orphanage where she used to live. After this my *tia* (auntie) looked after me, she also lived in the same house.

When I was about eleven years old my tia sent me to Belo Horizonte from Bahia because I was causing problems

215

for her. She left me in an orphanage called Cidade do Menor. But I didn't like it there because the older boys used to beat me up, and so I ran to the streets where I started to sniff glue. Then I telephoned my tia in Bahia and told her that I didn't like the Cidade do Menor and she came and got me.

A few months later, when I was twelve years old, she brought me back again to Belo Horizonte, only this time I stayed on the streets for almost a year. I stole a blanket from a balcony window and used to sleep in shop doorways and under freeways. Sometimes I was alone and other times I walked around with a group. Jose Roberto, who is on the farm also, was with me on the streets.

It was very difficult to sleep at night because other street kids would come by and wake you up. I sniffed glue and smoked marijuana to kill the hunger pangs. We stole people's wallets and took the money to a guy who used to sell drugs to us under a freeway in Pampulha.

Once I stole a necklace from a woman's neck and the police caught me. They demanded that I give them the necklace but I'd lost it while running. I was really frightened. But they let me go without beating me up.

It was horrible on the streets; there were fights and I was often filthy. Also I had a deep hate and jealousy of people who were rich, who had clothes, games, toys.

When I arrived at the farm last year I saw that things were different, and Jesus changed my life completely. The hate and jealousy disappeared, today I am happy with what I have and no longer resent what other people have that I don't. And I no longer think about stealing.

Some of us took a discipleship course last year and Sarah was talking to us about the gifts and fruits of the

Holy Spirit. Afterwards she prayed for us and I couldn't keep my mouth closed and I started to speak in tongues. Now I have such a desire to pray and to read the Bible.

Then at Christmastime Sally from Holy Trinity Brompton in London was here with a team, and she prayed for me. I started to shake and cry. Then I stopped crying and started to laugh and laugh. Suddenly I saw in my mind a picture of what I thought was heaven. It was a place full of clouds and beautiful trees and birds. There were lakes, waterfalls and animals. And as I was walking through this place I crossed over into what seemed to be hell. Everything was red and the trees were dead. The place with the waterfall was the same as I'd seen in heaven only the water was blood. I heard people screaming.

I had previously asked God to show me what heaven and hell looked like, so this was an answer to my prayer.

Another time when I was praying I saw in my mind a picture of a bright light and God said to me, 'Don't worry about your future because everything will be all right.' Then He showed me a house and on the house there was a sign with 'Study' written on it. I believe it has something to do with art and design and I believe this house is in England. I love to design and paint, especially nature.

Last year at school I was still causing problems, fighting with other boys and girls. But this year I've stopped. Jesus has given me enough love that I can control myself.

My tia came to the farm a couple of months ago. This was another answer to my prayers, and she told me that my mother is alive in Sao Paulo and that she is married with three more children. My tia is going to get my mother's address for me so that I can make contact with her soon!

*

His mother telephoned him and they spoke for the first time in over six years in July 1995. Oades is now working in the marketing department for the supermarket Bon Marche and living in the Casa Republic. He was baptised in water on August 27th 1995.

Eduardo Messias Merriel. Born: 28.12.80

I was born in Belo Horizonte fourteen years ago. My house has two rooms, a kitchen and a bedroom. My nine brothers and sisters and my parents all sleep in the same room.

There is a film that passes through my mind of when my mother and father took me to the FEBEM [the over-crowded government house for children], I was about two years old at the time. My aunt went and got me out and took me to live with her. But from that moment on I never wanted to live with my parents again. They rejected me, and I had a lot of anger inside as a result of this. I can be very nervous and easily irritated, especially when I came off drugs. So my aunt brought me up initially with my three cousins. They were poor too, only they lived in a different favela. I did eventually go back and live with my parents, only I never stayed for very long. From the age of eight I would spend my time between living on the streets and with my family. I got in with a bad crowd at school and I started to learn how to steal.

On the streets I knew Welbert. We were often together in the same gangs, Cabecao, Jacui. The leaders of the gangs would send us out to steal. I would rob wallets, watches and money from pedestrians. It was always easier to steal from people who wore baggy trousers with big

218

pockets, I would walk up close behind them and quick as a flash stick my hand inside their pockets and pull out their wallet. Then we would sell the goods to street sellers at the main bus station. With the money I'd buy drugs; marijuana, glue, solvent.

I nearly died once. Drugged out of my mind I crossed the main street, Antonio Carlos in the city centre, without looking and a car hit me. Apparently I flew before crashing to the tarmac. They took me to hospital to X-ray me. But I was out of my mind, crazy, screaming at everyone and they had to tie me down. Fortunately there was nothing seriously wrong and they let me go.

Then about two years ago I heard about Jesus for the first time, I was twelve years old. I would arrive at the Casa Aberta early in the morning, eat breakfast, brush my teeth and go to sleep on the carpet. Claudia, one of the workers there, used to stroke my head and talk to me. One day she spoke about the fiery furnace in Daniel, chapter 3, when King Nebuchadnezzar ordered three Jews to be thrown into the burning furnace because they refused to worship his golden idol. But they didn't die; in fact the king saw four men walking around inside the fire! The fourth man was an angel of God. When he ordered them out, the king and his governors saw to their amazement that not even their hair or clothes had been singed. They all praised the Jews' God.

This true story in the Bible really started to make me think for the first time. Then the next day I wanted to know all about Jesus. Although I still took drugs when back on the street at night, I started to desire to change. It was clear that I couldn't do this alone and that I needed Jesus to transform my life. One day I asked Him to come

219

into my life, I asked Him to forgive me for stealing and taking drugs. Soon after this I went to live on the farm. There my whole life started again. Instead of living on the streets, playing around, drugged out of my mind, I went to school, worked on the land, played sport and started to hear the Word of God. I knew all at once that the Word of God would enable me to be something in my life. My younger brother Cristiano had followed me to the streets and he too came to the farm.

After six months on the farm a pastor and his wife wanted to adopt us both. They had a small baby, Silas, and lived outside Belo Horizonte in Contagem. So Cristiano and I went to live with them. Everything went well at the beginning but then the pastor started to over-discipline us. He would spank us quite a lot. Cristiano and I made mistakes, but after seven months I didn't want to stay any more with them and we both ran away and went back to my parents' house.

But that didn't work out either for me. And although I found a job making furniture, the people I worked with were taking drugs. Also at home I was responsible for bathing my younger brothers and sisters and they'd complain about me to my mother and older sister and eventually they lost patience with me and my mother told me I'd be better off on the streets than with them. So pretty soon I went back on to the streets and stopped studying and working.

For two months I went back to my old life, stealing, fighting, taking drugs, only I didn't have sex like I'd had before. But I forgot all about Jesus, it was as though someone had come along and cleaned my memory of the Word of God I'd learned. The only thing I didn't forget was the music, the worship songs we sang at the farm and in church. Also there was always something inside me saying, 'Call Joao and Sarah, talk to them.' So every now and then I would telephone them at the farm for a chat, and they'd tell me that I had to make the decision to change, they couldn't make it for me. It was freezing at night on the streets this winter and three churches opened their doors at night for us to sleep inside. One night I told the people in the church that I was going to be a missionary for God. I was all dirty with no shoes on; I think they were surprised but they told me that to be a missionary is the very best thing to be.

I became ill with intoxication from the drugs I was taking. Around this time Selma (the co-ordinator) from the Casa Aberta called me at the church and asked me if I wanted to change my lifestyle. She told me to go to Casa Emmaus for a couple of nights and from there Joao would talk to me about the possibility of returning to the farm. So that's what I did.

My first week on the farm was a battle. I felt really tired and heavy all the time and only had bad thoughts of fighting and running away back to the streets.

Then Joao prayed for some of us and when it was my turn I wept and wept. It was great to be able to confess the things I'd done wrong and to be forgiven. I felt so light afterwards. The following Sunday nine of the teenagers on the farm were baptised in the swimming pool by Pastor Marcio from the Lagoinha church. I was one of them!

When I came out of the water it was as though the old Eduardo stayed behind in the water and a new me came out. For a week afterwards I felt so light and free, when I walked it was as though my feet didn't touch the ground.

I am going to be a missionary for God.

221

Messias Aleluia Rodrigues Ramos. Born: 16.9.80

My family used to live in an eight-roomed house here in Belo Horizonte. When I was five years old our neighbour started taking me to church every Sunday and there I learned how to pray. My mother practised Macumba. Then suddenly my father died and my mother sold the house and went to live in Sao Paulo. She left me and my brothers to live with my grandmother and aunt. But my two eldest brothers took me to live on the streets with them, I was seven years old at the time. For four years the street was my home. We slept on the pavements or in abandoned houses, travelled to other cities like Rio de Janeiro, Victoria, Sao Paulo, Cabo Frio, with stolen money. They used me to enter houses at night and let them in. I was very small, you see, at the time. We used to break into mansions in the rich area of the city.

During these four years I joined various gangs. At night there would often be guerras between the gangs. One time I was with the Graminha gang and we were having a party, when suddenly the Marcia gang attacked us with knives and fire. Fortunately during these guerras I was never knifed. But the police would always arrive and arrest some of us and beat us up bad. I went to prison three times. Once a girl in my gang had a fight with her boyfriend and he threatened to burn her. She didn't believe him. But when she was asleep he threw solvent over her and lit a match. It was terrible, she was toasted all over her head, shoulders and chest. Someone tried to put it out with water and she started to shrivel up. Believe it or not she survived, and after spending some time in hospital she returned to life on the streets. My two greatest friends were murdered; they were taken to the woods and killed.

I was hit by a car and broke my leg. Around this time a Christian woman adopted me, I was eleven years old at the time. But after a year I returned to the streets. I missed my brothers and found it difficult staying in a house. However, I wanted to change my lifestyle, I hadn't studied and was nearly thirteen years old. Then Youth With A Mission took me in to live in their restoration house. There I asked Jesus into my life. After a year and a half I ran away because I didn't like a discipline I was given.

Joining a gang we travelled to Victoria. There we broke into a tourist agency at night and stole money, uniforms, radios, many things. A woman living next door to the agency saw what was happening and called the police. I hid behind the counter but they caught me and beat me up and took us all to prison. The next day the judge let me go and they put me on a bus back to Belo Horizonte.

I joined another gang called Xuxa. We started stealing in *arrastao* [a large group running all together in a line] up the main streets in the city, pulling watches off people's wrists, handbags, jewellery, wallets. Then one day Silvania and some other workers from Crianca Feliz were on the streets and she told me to go to the Casa Aberta. So I went the next day. And immediately they asked me if I wanted to go to the farm. I couldn't decide. But they said if I wanted to go it had to be on that day, I couldn't go back to the streets. So I went to Casa Emmaus, and there I knew I really had to make some decisions about my life, once and for all, to follow Jesus. Because here on earth our time is short and it's easy indulging ourselves in a life that pleases the flesh, but at the end of time we are going to pay the price. I saw that the only way was to follow Jesus, the life I'd been living just left me with an empty heart. I was full of hate and any time anyone spoke to me I was aggressive with them and would fight easily.

Then one day I prayed for myself. I started observing Anderson [the street worker] and Welbert [an ex-street boy] in Casa Emmaus and I asked the Lord if I could be just like them. Anderson is calm and peaceful, not easily angered. The next day I felt different, the anger had gone. Someone irritated me, but I managed to be self-controlled. To begin with I was worried that people would think I'd gone wet, you know, too soft, but as I started to think about this I started to cry because it was from God. Then I came to the farm five months ago, and today I'm working for a large supermarket in the bakery section and at night I'm studying.

God has a purpose in my life, I don't know what it is yet. After I was baptised in water I felt lighter than ever. Before I walked around with a closed face, today I'm really happy, smiling and laughing all the time. Everyone who knew me before says I've really changed.

* * *

In the Bible whenever we read about a generation being persecuted it is because God has a plan for that generation and Satan tries to frustrate that plan, even though he can never stop the will or plan of God being realised. When God says He is going to do something, neither the negligence of man nor the strategies of Satan can stop it.

Abraham received a word from God that after four hundred years of slavery the people of God, the Hebrews, would be chosen by God to form a nation, Israel (Gen.15:13–14). There would be a leader, the precursor of Jesus the Saviour of all men, who by the power of God would lead them out of slavery and across the desert to a new land full of milk and honey.

After four hundred years Satan found the king of Egypt, Pharaoh, who was threatened by the prophecy among the Hebrews that God would raise in that generation of slaves a prophet to be their leader and liberator. Through Pharaoh, Satan tried to prevent the generation of boys surviving and attempted to kill the boy who would be Moses. But two midwives, Shiphrah and Puah, who feared God more than they feared the king, risking their lives, disobeyed Pharaoh and saved many boys including Moses. Eventually Pharaoh gave the order that every Hebrew boy born should be thrown into the Nile, and many baby boys were murdered. But God showed His majesty and greatness when the very person who was being used by Satan ended up adopting Moses into his own household. Moses, who at three months old had been placed in a basket among the reeds along the bank of the Nile by his mother, was found by Pharaoh's daughter (Exodus 1 and 2).

This also shows God's power and sense of humour towards Satan, a fallen creature who rebelled against God and who is already condemned (Rev. 20:7–10).

Throughout the Old Testament there are around three hundred prophecies before the coming of the Messiah, the Lamb of God who would take away the sins of the world. In the same way Satan used an insecure king, Herod, leader of Judea, who with the news that the prophecies had been fulfilled and that the 'king of the Jews' had been born in Bethlehem, had all the little boys aged two and under killed in the vicinity. However, Joseph and Mary had already escaped with baby Jesus to Egypt because an angel of the Lord had previously warned Joseph in a dream (Matt. 2).

In the same way today, the Word says that the Gospel should be taken to every nation, tribe, people and language (Rev.7:9, Matt.28:18–20), and Satan is trying to prevent that by persecuting the children, using them as never before: some are killed so that their organs can be sold; millions die through lack of food; others are the victims of war; some are killed to be used as sacrifices in satanic practices.

In Brazil alone there are more than 1,200,000 abortions per year and 200,000 teenage girls die as a result of malpractice (statistics from the Instituto Brasileiro de Geografica e Estatisticas).

We believe that this is a generation from which God wants to raise up prophets. In the book of Amos, chapter 3, verse 7, we read, 'Surely the Sovereign Lord does nothing without revealing his plan to his servants the prophets.' The challenge God is giving the Church today is to stand up against this wave of injustice of demonic persecution against the children in the whole world. The Church today has to pray and act for the rights of these children to live a worthy life, with the liberty to know Jesus as their Lord and Saviour. It is the local church which has to pass this baton to the children, not only save them but disciple and guide them in the way of the Lord so that they can run a good distance of the race.

Because of this, and as part of the Church and members of the body of Christ, we stand against this demonic wave of injustice, destruction, murder and violence threatening God's children. We commit ourselves to undo the work that Satan has done, through the power of Jesus Christ, and to reconstruct the kingdom of God in their lives. And when the will of God is done, and the Gospel preached throughout the whole world, then Jesus will come.

Donations and correspondence may be sent to:

Ministerio Programa Crianca Feliz
Cx. Postal 370
Belo Horizonte, MG
CEP 30.161-970 Brazil
Tel: (031) 673-1266 Fax: (031) 673 1306

Happy Child Mission
Old Tunmore Farm
The Street
West Horsley
Surrey KT24 6BB
England
Registered Charity No: 1042236

A/C No. 91790358
Midland Bank plc
PO Box 160
Guildford
Surrey GU1 3YU
England

Happy Child Mission
1415 Northridge
Carrolton, Texas 75006
USA
Registered Charity No: EIN 75-2489963

A/C No. 1291883198
Nations Bank of Texas, N.A.
3601 N. Josey Lane
Carrolton, Texas 75007
USA